MEN OF THE BIBLE

MEN OF THE BIBLE

Therefore, seeing we also are compassed about with so great a cloud of witnesses, leaving behind all the weight of the sin which surrounds us, let us run with patience the race that is set before us – Hebrews 12:1

DWIGHT L. MOODY

We love hearing from our readers. Please contact us at www.anekopress.com/questions-comments with any questions, comments, or suggestions.

Men of the Bible – Dwight L. Moody

First edition published 1898

Originally published by
The Bible Institute Colportage Association,
829 La Salle Avenue, Chicago

Cover Design: Natalia Hawthorne

Cover Photography: BCFC/Shutterstock

Editors: Sheila Wilkinson and Paul Miller

Aneko Press

www.anekopress.com

Aneko Press, Life Sentence Publishing, and our logos are trademarks of

Life Sentence Publishing, Inc.
203 E. Birch Street
P.O. Box 652
Abbotsford, WI 54405

RELIGION / Christian Life / Spiritual Growth

Paperback ISBN: 978-1-62245-528-7

eBook ISBN: 978-1-62245-529-4

10 9 8 7 6 5 4 3

Available where books are sold

Contents

Chapter 1

Abraham

Faith and Obedience

Many people are afraid of the will of God, but one of the sweetest lessons we can learn as Christians is to surrender our wills to God, allowing Him to plan and rule our lives. If I know my own mind and could plan my life, what would I do? If an angel would come from the throne of God and tell me that I could have my will done all the days of my life and that everything I wished for would be carried out, or else I could refer it back to God and let God's will be done in me and through me, what would I do? I think in an instant I would say, "Let the will of God be done."

I cannot look into the future. I don't know what is going to happen tomorrow. In fact, I don't know what might happen before tonight, so I cannot choose for myself as well as God can choose for me. It is much better to surrender my will to God's will.

Abraham learned this himself. He surrendered to

God in four different areas of his life, and these four surrenders give us a good key to his life.

Abraham's First Surrender

In the first place, Abraham was called to give up his family and his native country and to go out, not knowing where he was to go.

While others were busy building up Babylon, God called this man out of that nation of the Chaldeans. He lived down near the mouth of the Euphrates, maybe three hundred miles south of Babylon, when he was called to go into a land that he perhaps had never heard of before, and he was told to possess that land.

In the twelfth chapter of Genesis we read of a promise that God made to Abram:

> *But the LORD had said unto Abram, Depart out of thy country and from thy nature and from thy father's house unto a land that I will show thee. And I will make of thee a great nation, and I will bless thee and make thy name great; and thou shalt be a blessing. And I will bless those that bless thee and curse those that curse thee, and in thee shall all families of the earth be blessed. So Abram departed, as the Lord had spoken unto him, and Lot went with him, and Abram was seventy-five years old when he departed out of Haran.* (Genesis 12:1-4)

God had first told Abram to leave Ur of the Chaldees

several years before this.[1] He went to Haran, which is about halfway between the valley of the Euphrates and the valley of the Jordan. God had called him into the land of the Canaanites, and he went halfway and stayed there. We do not know how long he stayed there, but it was probably about five years.

I believe there are a great many Christians who are what we might call *Haran Christians.* They go to Haran, and there they stay. They only half obey. They are not fully obedient. How was it that God got him out of Haran? Abram's father died. The first call was to leave Ur of the Chaldees and go into Canaan, but instead of going all the way, they stopped halfway. It was affliction that drove Abram out of Haran.[2] Many of us bring afflictions on ourselves because we are not completely living for the Lord. We do not always obey Him fully. God had plans He wanted to work out through Abram, and He could not work them out as long as he was at

---

1 Editor's note: Some believe Terah, Abram's father, also received a call from God and that is why Genesis 11:31 says that Terah led Abram out of Ur. Others contend that Terah did not receive a call but took his family north to Haran anyway. However, there is no Scripture indicating either of these assumptions. Scripture repeatedly says that God called Abram out of Ur. Note Genesis 15:7 and Nehemiah 9:7. Acts 7:2-4 particularly gives credence to the fact that God called Abram while he was in Ur. Very likely, when Abram obeyed God and left Ur, Terah, as head of the family, went along. Genesis 12:1-4 begins with the past tense verb *had*, so this call likely occurred prior to 11:31.

2 Editor's note: Though the author said affliction "drove" Abram out of Haran, Terah may still have served idols (Joshua 24:2). Therefore, God could not allow him to enter the promised land, so He let Abram stay in Haran until his father died. Then he was free to go on to Canaan. If this is so, the time spent in Haran was not in disobedience, but maybe even obedience. Scripture does not say that Abram disobeyed God by staying in Haran. Whether or not Abram was afflicted, however, does not negate the fact that God uses these troubling times to move us onward, as stated in James 1:1-13.

Haran. Affliction came, and then we find that he left Haran and started for the promised land.

There is just one word here about Lot: *and Lot went with him*. That is the key, you might say, to Lot's life. He was a weaker character than Abram, and he followed his uncle.

When they reached the land that God had promised to give him, Abram found it already inhabited by great and warlike nations – not by one nation, but by a number of nations.[3] What could he, a solitary man in that land, do? Not only was his faith tested by finding the land inhabited by other strong and hostile nations, but he had only been there a little while when a great famine came upon the land.

No doubt Abram experienced a great conflict in his heart, and he probably said to himself, "What does this mean? Here I am, thirteen hundred miles away from my own land and surrounded by a warlike people. Not only that, but a famine has come, and I must get out of this country."

I don't believe that God sent Abram down to Egypt. I think He was only testing him so that he might be drawn nearer to God in his time of darkness and trouble. I believe that many times of trouble and sorrow are permitted to come to us so that we may see the face of God – that we might be compelled to trust in Him alone.

---

3 Though Genesis 12:6 says that *the Canaanite was then in the land*, *Canaanite* is often a general term used for all the nations that inhabited that land.

Abraham's Second Surrender

Abram became rich, but we don't hear of any altar after he left Canaan; in fact, we hear of no altar at Haran, and we hear of no altar in Egypt. When he came up with Lot out of Egypt, they had great possessions. They had increased in wealth, and their herds had multiplied until there was conflict among their herdsmen.

Now Abram's character shines again. He could have said that he had a right to the best of everything because he was older and because Lot probably would not have been worth anything if it had not been for Abram's help. But instead of standing up for his right to choose the best of the land, he surrendered that right and said to his nephew, "Take your choice. If you go to the right hand, I will take the left; or if you prefer the left hand, then I will go to the right."

Here is where Lot made his mistake. If there was ever a man under the sun who needed Abram's counsel, prayers, and influence, it was Lot. He needed to be surrounded by Abram's friends. Lot was just one of those weak characters who needed to be bolstered up, but his covetous eye looked upon the well-watered plains of the Jordan Valley that reached out toward Sodom, and he chose them. He was influenced by what he saw. He walked by sight instead of by faith.

I think that is where a great many Christians make their mistake – they walk by sight instead of by faith. If Lot had stopped to think, he might have realized that it would be disastrous to him and his family to go anywhere near Sodom. Abram and Lot both must have known about the wickedness of those cities on the plains. Although they were rich and there was the chance of making money, Lot should have kept his family out of that wicked city. However, his eyes fell upon the well-watered plains, and he pitched his tent toward Sodom and separated from Abram.

Notice that after Abram allowed Lot to have his choice, Lot left for the plains, and God had Abram alone for the first time. His father had died at Haran, and he had left his brother Nahor there. Now, after Lot left him, Abram moved to Haran and built an altar to the Lord. *Hebron* means "communion." It is here that God came to Abram and said:

> *Lift up now thine eyes and look from the place where thou art towards the Aquilon and to the Negev and to the east and to the west; for all the land which thou seest, to thee will I give it and to thy seed forever. And I will make thy seed as the dust of the earth, so that if someone could number the dust of the earth, then shall thy seed also be numbered. Arise, walk through the land in the length of it and in the breadth of it, for I must give it unto thee.*
>
> *Then Abram removed his tent and came and dwelt among the terebinth trees of Mamre, which is in Hebron, and built there an altar unto the Lord.* (Genesis 13:14-18)

It is astonishing how far you can see in that country. God took Moses up on Mount Pisgah and showed him the promised land. In the land of Israel a few years ago, I found that from the Mount of Olives I could look over and see the Mediterranean Sea. I could look into the Jordan Valley and see the Dead Sea. From the plains of Sharon, I could look up to Mount Lebanon and Mount Hermon, way beyond Nazareth. With the naked eye, you can see almost the entire length and breadth of that country.

So when God said to Abram that he should look to the north, and as far as he could see, he could have the land, and then look to the south with its well-watered plains that Lot coveted, and then look to the east and the west, from the sea to the Euphrates, then God gave His friend Abram a clear title to the land with no conditions whatever. God said, "I will give it all to you."

Lot chose all he could get, but it was not much. Abram let God choose for him, and God gave him all the land. Lot had no security for his choice, and he soon lost it all. Abram's right to his land was maintained undisputed by God, the giver.

Do you know that the children of Israel never had faith enough to take possession of all that land as far as the Euphrates? If they had, Nebuchadnezzar would probably have never come and taken them captive. But that was God's offer; He said to Abram, *Unto thy seed shall I give this land, from the river of Egypt unto the great river, the river Euphrates* (Genesis 15:18).

From that time on, God enlarged Abram's tents. He enriched His promises and gave Abram much more than He had promised down in the valley of the Euphrates when He first called him out. It is very interesting to see how God kept adding to the promise for the benefit of His friend Abram.

Let us consider Lot now and see what he gained by making the choice he did. I believe that we can find five thousand Lots to every one Abram today. People are constantly walking by sight, lured by the temptations of people and of the world. Men are very anxious to get their sons into lucrative positions, although it may be disastrous to their character. It can ruin them morally and religiously and in every other way. The glitter of this world seems to attract them. Someone has said that Abram was a farsighted man and Lot was a shortsighted man, for Lot's eye fell on the land immediately around him. There is one thing that we are quite sure of – he was so shortsighted that he soon lost his possessions. We find that people who are constantly taking the quickest or easiest way out are often disappointed.

I have no doubt that the men of Sodom told Lot that he was a much shrewder man than his uncle Abram, and that if he lived twenty-five years longer, he would be the richer of the two. They might have told him that by coming into Sodom, he could sell his cattle and sheep and goats and whatever else he had for large sums and get a much better deal than Abram could back on the plains of Mamre.

For a while, Lot might have made money very quickly and might have become a very successful man. If we had gone into Sodom a little while before destruction came, we might have found that Lot owned some of the best corner lots in town, and Mrs. Lot moved in what they called the *bon-ton* society – or the elite and sophisticated class of people. We would have found that she was at the theater two or three nights a week. If they played cards, she probably played as well as anybody, and her daughters may have danced as well as any other Sodomites.

We find Lot sitting in the gates, getting on amazingly well. He might have been one of the principal men in the city; maybe he was Judge Lot or the Honorable Lot of Sodom. If there had been a Congress in those days, he may have run for a seat in Congress, or they might have elected him mayor of Sodom. He was getting on amazingly well and was wonderfully prosperous; but after a while, war was upon them. If you decide to live in Sodom, you must take part in Sodom's judgment when it comes, for it is bound to come. The battle turned against those five cities of the plain, and they took Lot and his wife and all that they had. One man escaped and ran to Hebron and told Abram what had taken place. Abram took his servants – three hundred and eighteen of them – and went after these victorious kings. He soon returned with all the plunder and all the prisoners, including Lot and his family.

Abraham's Third Surrender

On Abram's way back with the plunder, one of the strangest scenes of history occurs. Abram met Melchizedek, who brought out bread and wine. The priestly king blessed the father of the faithful, and the old king of peace blessed Abram. Then Abram met the king of Sodom, who said to Abram, "You take the money, and I will take the people."

Abram replied, *I will not take from a thread even to a shoelatchet; I will not take any thing that is thine, lest thou should say, I have made Abram rich* (Genesis 14:23).

This was another surrender – a temptation to get rich at the hands of the king of Sodom; but the king of Salem had blessed him, so this world did not tempt him. It tempted Lot, and no doubt Lot thought Abram made a great mistake when he refused to take this wealth; but Abram would not touch a thing. He spurned it and turned from it. He had the world under his feet. He was living for another world. He would not be enriched from such a source.

Each one of us is met by the prince of this world and the Prince of Peace. The one tempts us with wealth, pleasure, and ambition, but our Prince and Priest is ready to help and strengthen us in the hour of temptation.

A friend of mine told me some years ago that his wife was very fond of painting, but for a long time he could not see any beauty in her paintings. They all looked blurry to him. One day his eyes troubled him, and he went to see an optometrist. The man looked in amazement at him and said, "You have what we call a short eye and a long eye, and that makes everything blurry."

The optometrist gave him some glasses that fit him, and he could see clearly. Then he said that he understood why it was that his wife was so carried away with art. He built an art gallery and filled it with beautiful things, because everything looked so beautiful to him after he got his eye problem straightened out.

There are many people who have a long eye and

a short eye, and they make miserable work of their Christian life. They keep one eye on the eternal city and the other eye on the well-watered plains of Sodom. That was the way it was with Lot; he had a short eye and a long eye. It would be pretty hard work to believe that Lot was saved if it were not for the New Testament, but we read that God *delivered just Lot, who was persecuted by those abominable people because of their nefarious conversation; (for that righteous man dwelling among them, in seeing and hearing, afflicted his righteous soul from day to day with the deeds of those unjust people)* (2 Peter 2:7-8). Lot's soul was vexed. He had a righteous soul, but he had a stormy life. He didn't have peace and joy and victory like Abram.

After Abram had given up the wealth of Sodom that was offered to him, God came and enlarged his borders again; He enlarged the promise. God said, *I am thy shield, and thy exceeding great reward* (Genesis 15:1).

Abram might have thought that these kings he had defeated might get other kings and other armies to come. He might have thought of himself as a solitary man with only three hundred and eighteen men, so he might have feared he would be swept from the face of the earth. But the Lord came and said, *Fear not, Abram.* That is the first time those often repeated words *fear not* occur in the Bible. *Fear not, Abram, I am thy shield, and thy exceeding great reward* (Genesis 15:1).

I would rather have that promise than all the armies of earth and all the navies of the world to protect me – to have the God of heaven for my Protector. God was teaching Abram that He was to be his Friend and his

Shield, if he would surrender himself wholly to His keeping and trust in His goodness. That is what we need – to surrender ourselves up to God, fully and entirely.

In Colorado, the superintendent of some works told me of a miner who was promoted. He went to the superintendent and said, "There is a man who has seven children, and I have only three; he is having a hard struggle. Don't promote me, but promote him."

I know of nothing that speaks louder for Christ and Christianity than to see a man or woman giving up what they call their rights for others, and *with honour preferring one another* (Romans 12:10).

We find that Abram was constantly surrendering his own selfish interests and trusting God. What was the result? Of all the men who ever lived, he is the most renowned. He never did anything the world would call great. The largest army he ever mustered was three hundred and eighteen men. How Alexander the Great would have sneered at such an army as that! How Caesar would have looked down on such an army! How Napoleon would have curled his lip as he thought of Abram with an army of three hundred and eighteen!

We are not told that he was a great astronomer. We are not told that he was a great scientist. We are not told that he was a great statesman, or anything this world calls great, but there was one thing he could do – he could live an unselfish life and in honor waive his rights. In that way he became the friend of God, and in that way he has become immortal.

There is no name in history as well known as the name of Abram. Even Christ is not more widely known, for the Muslims, the Persians, and the Egyptians make a great deal of Abram. His name has been favorably known in Damascus for centuries and centuries. God promised him that great men, warriors, kings, and emperors would spring from his loins.

Was there ever a nation that has turned out such men? Think of Moses, Joseph, Joshua, Caleb, Samuel, David, Solomon, and Elisha. Think of Elijah, Daniel, Isaiah, and all the other wonderful Bible characters who have descended from this man! Then think of Peter, James, John, Paul, and John the Baptist – a mighty army. No one can number the multitude of wonderful men who have originated from this one man who was called out of the land of the Chaldeans, unknown and probably an idolater when God called him; yet God has literally fulfilled His promise that through him He would bless all the nations of the earth – all because Abram surrendered himself completely to let God bless him.

Abraham's Fourth Surrender[4]

The last surrender is perhaps the most touching and the hardest of all to understand. Perhaps he could not have endured it until the evening of life. God had been taking him along, step by step, until he had reached a

4 Editor's note: By now, Abraham's faith was firmly and deeply rooted. Hebrews 11:17-19 gives us a slightly different picture than the author is painting in this section, in that Abraham did not think the Lord was forsaking His previous promises regarding his son, but thought that the Lord would instead raise his son again after Abraham killed him. If anything, this only gives us an even more profound glimpse into Abraham's faith, as he rightly figured that the Lord was testing him and that the Lord was and always will be completely faithful to His word. Neither does scripture give any indication that Abraham struggled to give up his son, but simply and willingly did as the Lord commanded him.

place where he had learned to fully obey whatever God told him to do. I believe the world has yet to see what God will do with the man who is perfectly surrendered to Him. Next to God's own Son, Abraham was perhaps the man who came nearest to this standard.

For twenty-five years, Abraham had been in the promised land without the promised heir. God had promised that He would bless all the nations of the earth through him, and yet He did not give him a son. Abraham's faith almost staggered a number of times. Ishmael was born, but God set aside the son of the bondwoman, for he was not to be the ancestor of the Son of God. God was setting Abraham apart in order to prepare the way for His own Son, and at last, a messenger came down from heaven to Hebron and told Abraham in his old age that he would have a son.

It seemed too good to be true. He struggled to believe it, but at the appointed time Isaac was born into that family. I don't believe there was ever a child born into the world that caused so much joy in the home as Isaac did in Abraham's heart and home. How Abraham and that old mother, Sarah, must have adored that child! How their eyes feasted on him!

But just when the boy was growing into manhood, Abraham received another very strange command for another surrender – that of his only son. Perhaps he was making an idol of that boy and thought more of him than he did of the God who gave him. There must be no idol in the heart if we are going to do the will of God on earth.

I can imagine that one night the old patriarch went

to bed worn out and weary. The boy had gone fast to sleep, when suddenly a heavenly messenger came and told Abraham that he must take that boy off to a mountain that God was to show him and offer him as a sacrifice. No more sleep that night! If we had looked into that tent the next morning, I can imagine we would have seen the servants flying around and preparing for the master's long journey. Maybe Abraham kept the secret locked up in his heart and didn't even tell Sarah or Isaac. He didn't tell the servants, even the faithful servant Eliezer, what was to take place.

About eight o'clock in the morning we might have seen those four men – Abraham, Isaac, and the two young men with them – begin the long journey. Once in a while, Abraham might have turned his head aside and wiped away a tear. He wouldn't want Isaac to see what a terrible struggle was going on within him. It was a hard battle to give up his will and surrender that boy, the idol of his life. Oh, how he loved him!

I can imagine the first night. The boy soon fell asleep, tired and weary from the hot day's journey, but the old man couldn't sleep. I can see him look into the face of the innocent boy and say, "Soon my boy will be gone, and I will be returning without him."

Perhaps most of the night his voice would have been heard in prayer as he cried to God to help him; and as God had helped him in the past, so God helped him that night.

The next day they journeyed on, and again Abraham suffered a terrible conflict. Again he brushed away a tear. Perhaps Isaac saw it and thought, "Father is going away to meet his God, and the angels may come down and talk with him as at Hebron. That is what he is so distressed about."

The second night came, and the old man looked into that face every hour of the night. He slept a little, but not much, and the next morning at family worship, he broke down. He could not finish his prayer.

They journeyed on that day – it was a long day – and the old patriarch said, "This is the last day I am to have my boy with me. Tomorrow I must offer him up; tomorrow I will be without the son of my bosom."

The third night came, and what a night it must have been! I can imagine he didn't eat or sleep that night. Nothing was going to break his fast, and every hour of the night he went to look into the face of that boy. Once in a while he bent over and kissed him and said, "O Isaac, how can I give you up?"

Then the morning broke. What a morning it must have been for that father! He didn't eat. He tried to pray, but his voice faltered. After breakfast they started on their journey again. He had not gone far before he lifted up his eyes and saw Mount Moriah. His heart began to beat quickly. He said to the two young men, "You stay here, and I will go over there with my son."

Then, as father and son went up Mount Moriah with the wood, the fire, and the knife, the boy suddenly turned to his father and said, "Father, where is the lamb? We haven't any offering, Father." It was a common thing for Isaac to see his father offer up a victim, but there was no lamb this time.

Consider how prophetic that answer was when

Abraham turned and said, *My son, God will provide himself a lamb for a burnt offering* (Genesis 22:8). I don't know that Abraham understood the full meaning of it, but a few hundred years later, God did provide a sacrifice right there. Mount Moriah and Mount Calvary are close together, and God's Son was provided as a sacrifice for the world.

On Mount Moriah, this father and son began to roll up the stones, and together they built the altar. They laid the wood on it, and everything was ready for the victim. Isaac looked around to see where the lamb was, and the father could keep it from the son no longer. Abraham said, "My boy, sit down here close to the altar, and let me tell you something."

Then that old white-haired patriarch might have put his arm around his son and told how God came to him in the land of the Chaldeans. He might have told Isaac the story of his whole life, and how by one promise after another, God had kept enlarging the promised blessings – that He would bless all the nations of the earth through him. Isaac was to be the heir, but Abraham said, "My son, the last night I was at home, God came to me in the late hours of the night and told me to bring you here and offer you up as a sacrifice. I don't understand what it means, but I can tell you one thing – it is much harder for me to offer you than it would be for me to be sacrificed myself."

There was a time when I used to think more of the love of Jesus Christ than of God the Father. I used to think of God as a stern judge on the throne from whose wrath Jesus Christ had saved me. It seems to me now that my idea of God could not have been more wrong.

Since I have become a father, I have made the discovery that it takes more love and self-sacrifice for the father to give the son up than it does for the son to die. Is a father on earth a true father if he would not rather suffer than to see his child suffer? Do you think that it did not cost God something to redeem this world? It cost God the most precious possession He ever had. When God gave His Son, He gave all, and yet He gave Him freely for you and me.

I can imagine that Abraham talked to Isaac and told him how hard it was to offer him up. "But God has commanded it," he said, "and I surrender my will to God's will. I don't understand it, but I believe that God will be able to raise you up, and maybe He will."

I imagine they fell on their faces and prayed together. After prayer, I can see that old father take his boy to his chest and embrace him for the last time. He kissed and kissed him. Then he took those hands that were so innocent and bound them. He bound Isaac's feet, tied him up, laid him on the altar, and gave him one last kiss. Then he took the knife and raised his hand. No sooner was the hand lifted than a voice from heaven called, *Abraham, Abraham . . . lay not thine hand upon the lad* (Genesis 22:11-12).

Do you remember when Christ said, *Abraham rejoiced to see my day, and he saw it and was glad* (John 8:56)? I have an idea that God then and there lifted the curtain of time for Abraham. He looked down into the future and saw God's Son coming up Calvary, bearing his sins and the sins of all future generations. God gave him that secret and told him how His Son was to come into the world and take away his sins.

Now, my friends, whenever God has been calling me to higher service, there has always been a conflict with my will. I have fought against it, but God's will has been done instead of mine. When I came to Jesus Christ, I had a terrible battle to surrender my will and to accept God's will. When I gave up business, I had another battle for three months; I fought against it. It was a terrible battle, but many times I have thanked God that I gave up my will and accepted His will.

Then there was another time when God was calling me into higher service – to go out and preach the gospel all over the land instead of staying in Chicago. I fought against it for months, but the best thing I ever did was when I surrendered my will and let the will of God be done in me. Because Abraham obeyed God and did not even hold back his only child, God enlarged His promises once again:

> *And the angel of the LORD called unto Abraham out of heaven the second time and said, By myself I have sworn, said the LORD, for because thou hast done this thing and hast not withheld thy son, thine only son; that in blessing I will bless thee and in multiplying I will multiply thy seed as the stars of the heaven and as the sand which is upon the sea shore; and thy seed shall possess the gates of his enemies; and in*

> *thy seed shall all the Gentiles of the earth be blessed because thou hast hearkened unto my voice.* (Genesis 22:15-18)

If you take my advice, you will have no will other than God's will. Make a full and complete surrender, and the sweet messages of heaven will come to you. God will whisper into your soul the secrets of heaven.

After Abraham obeyed God, then it was that God may have told His friend all about His Son. If we make a full surrender, God will give us something better than we have ever known before. We will get a new vision of Jesus Christ, and we will thank God not only in this life, but in the life to come. May God help each and every one of us to make a full, complete, and unconditional surrender to Him – now and forever.

Chapter 2

Moses

God's Voice

A great deal more room is given in Scripture to the call of men to God's work than there is to their end. For instance, we don't know where or how Isaiah died, but we know a great deal about God's call to him when he saw God on high and lifted up on His throne. I suppose it is true today that hundreds of young men and women who are listening for a call and really want to know what their life's mission is find it the greatest problem they ever had. Some don't know what profession or work to take up, so I would like to consider the call of Moses and see if we cannot draw some lessons from it.

You may remember when God met Moses at the burning bush and called him to do as great a work as any man has ever been called to in this world. Moses thought that the Lord had made a mistake and that he was not the right man for the job. He asked, *Who am I that I should go unto Pharaoh and that I should bring forth the sons of Israel out of Egypt?* (Exodus 3:11). He was very small in his own estimation. Forty years earlier, he had started out as many others have done. He thought he was pretty well-equipped for service. He had been in the schools of the Egyptians. He had been in the palaces of Egypt, where he had moved among the elite, sophisticated society. Undoubtedly, he had all the advantages any man could have when he started out, without calling on the God of Abraham for wisdom and guidance; yet he broke down.

How many men have started in some profession and failed in it? They haven't heard the voice of God. They haven't waited upon God for instruction.

I suppose Moses thought that the children of Israel would be greatly honored to know that a prince of the kingdom was going to take up their cause. You will remember, though, how he lost his temper and killed the Egyptian, and on the next day, when he interfered in a quarrel between two Hebrews, they wanted to know who had made him judge and ruler over them. He had to flee into the desert, and he remained there for forty years, hidden away (Exodus 2:14-15; Acts 7:23-36). Moses killed the Egyptian and lost his influence through that action. Murder for liberty; wrong for right. It was a poor way to reform abuses, and Moses needed training.

Forty years was a long time for God to keep him in His school. It was a long time for a man to wait in the prime of his life – from forty to eighty. Moses had been brought up with all the luxuries that Egypt could give him, and now he was a shepherd. In the sight of the Egyptians, a shepherd was an abomination. I think Moses started out with a bigger head than heart, and I believe that is the reason so many fail. They have big heads and little hearts.

If a man has a shriveled-up heart and a big head, he is a monster. Perhaps Moses looked down on the Hebrews. Many people start out with the idea that they are great and other people are small, and they think they are going to bring others up on the high level with themselves. God never yet used a man like that. Perhaps Moses was a slow scholar in God's school, so God had to keep him there for forty years.

Now he was ready. He was just the man God wanted, and God called him. Moses asked, *Who am I?* He was very small in his own eyes – just small enough so God could use him.

If you had asked the Egyptians who he was, they would have said he was the biggest fool in the world. They would have said, "Look at the opportunity that man had! He could have been commander of the whole Egyptian army. He could have been on the throne, swaying the scepter over the whole world if he hadn't identified himself with those poor, miserable Hebrews! Think what an opportunity he has lost and what a privilege he has thrown away!"

Moses had dropped out of the public mind for forty years, and they didn't know what had become of him; but God had His eye upon him. He was the very man of all others whom God wanted, and when he met God with that question, *Who am I?* it didn't matter who he was, but who his God was.

When people learn the lesson that they are nothing and God is everything, there is not a position in which God cannot use them. It was not Moses who accomplished that great work of redemption, for he was only the instrument in God's hand. God could have spoken to Pharaoh without Moses. He could have spoken in a voice of thunder and broken the heart of Pharaoh with one speech if He had wanted to, but He condescended to take up a human agent and use him. He could have sent the angel Gabriel down, but he knew that Moses was the man wanted above all others, so He called him.

God uses men to speak to men. He works through mediators. He could have accomplished the exodus of the children of Israel in a moment, but instead He chose to send a lonely and despised shepherd to work out His purpose through pain and disappointment. That was God's way in the Old Testament and in the New. He sent His own Son in the likeness of sinful flesh to be the mediator between God and man.

Moses went on making excuses. He asked, *When I come unto the sons of Israel and say unto them, The God of your fathers has sent me unto you, and if they say to me, What is his name? What shall I say unto them?* (Exodus 3:13). I suppose he remembered how he failed when he went before he was sent that other time, and he was afraid of failure again. A man who has failed once is always afraid he will fail again. He loses confidence in himself. It is a good thing to lose confidence in ourselves in order to gain confidence in God.

The Lord said, *I AM (YHWH) has sent me unto you* (Exodus 3:14).

Someone has said that God gave him a blank check, and all Moses had to do was fill it out from that time on. When he wanted to bring water out of the rock, all he had to do was fill out the check. When he wanted bread, all he had to do was fill out the check, and the bread came. He had a rich banker. God had taken him into partnership with Himself. God had made him His heir, and all he had to do was look to Him, and he got all he wanted.

Yet he seemed to back away and make another excuse. He said, *They will not believe me, nor hearken unto my voice* (Exodus 4:1). He was afraid of the Israelites, as well as of Pharaoh. He knew how hard it was to get even your friends to believe in you.

Now, if God has sent us with a message, it is not for us to say whether or not others will believe it. We cannot make them believe. If I have been sent by God to make people believe, He will give me power to make them believe. This is the work of the Holy Spirit. We cannot persuade men and overcome skepticism and infidelity unless we are baptized with the Holy Spirit and with power.

God told Moses that they would believe him, that he would succeed, and that he would bring the children of Israel out of bondage; but Moses seemed to distrust the God who had spoken to him.

Then the Lord asked, *What is that in thy hand?* (Exodus 4:2). Moses had a rod or staff, a sort of shepherd's crook, which he had made when he had needed something that would serve him in the desert.

"It is only a rod," Moses answered.

God explained to Moses that with that rod he would deliver the children of Israel. God showed Moses that the rod would help Israel believe that God was with him. *Therefore they will believe that the LORD God of their fathers, the God of Abraham, the God of Isaac, and the God of Jacob, has appeared unto thee* (Exodus 4:5). When God Almighty linked Himself to that rod, it was worth more than all the armies the world had ever seen. Look and see how that rod did its work. It brought up the plagues of flies and the thunderstorm, and it turned the water into blood. It was not Moses, however, nor his rod that did the work, but it was the God of the rod – the God of Moses. As long as God was with him, he could not fail.

Sometimes God's servants seem to fail. When Herod beheaded John the Baptist, it looked as if John's mission was a failure. But was it? The voice that rang through the valley of the Jordan rings through the whole world today. You can still hear its echo upon the mountains and the valleys: *It is expedient unto him to increase, but unto me, to decrease* (John 3:30). John the Baptist held up Jesus Christ and introduced Him to the world, and Herod didn't have power to behead John until his life's work had been accomplished.

Stephen only preached one sermon that we know of, and that was to the Sanhedrin; but that sermon has been preached again and again all over the world (Acts 7). After his death came Paul, the greatest preacher the world has seen since Christ left this earth. If a man is sent by Jehovah, there is no such thing as failure. Was Christ's life a failure? See how His parables travel across the earth today. It looked as if the apostles had failed, but see how much has been accomplished. If you read the book of Acts, you will see that every seeming failure in Acts was turned into a great victory. Moses wasn't going to fail, although Pharaoh asked with contempt, *Who is the LORD, that I should hearken to his voice to let Israel go?* (Exodus 5:2). He found out who God was. He found out that there was a God.

Moses made another excuse, saying, *I am slow of speech and of a slow tongue* (Exodus 4:10). He said he was not an orator.

My friends, we have too many orators. I am sick and tired of silver-tongued orators. I used to regret that I couldn't be an orator. I thought, "Oh, if I could only have the gift of speech like some men!" I have heard men with a smooth flow of language take the audience captive, but they came and they went. Their voice was like the air. There was no power behind it. They trusted in their eloquence and their fine speeches. That is what Paul was thinking about when he wrote to the Corinthians: *My speech and my preaching was not with enticing words of human wisdom, but in demonstration of the Spirit and of power, that your faith should not be founded in the wisdom of men, but in the power of God* (1 Corinthians 2:4-5).

Consider a witness in court who tries out his oratorical powers on the witness stand; see how quickly the judge will rule him out. It is the one who tells the plain, simple truth who will have the most influence with the jury.

Suppose Moses had prepared a speech for Pharaoh, had his hair all smoothly brushed, and had stood before a mirror or had gone to a speech instructor to be taught how to make an oratorical speech, complete with gestures. Suppose he had buttoned his coat, slipped one hand inside, struck an attitude, and began: "The God of our fathers, the God of Abraham, Isaac, and Jacob, has commanded me to come into the presence of the noble king of Egypt."

I think they would have taken his head right off! They had some Egyptians who could be as eloquent as Moses. It was not eloquence they lacked. When you see a man in the pulpit trying to show off his eloquence, he is making a fool of himself and trying to make a fool of the people. Moses was slow of speech, but he had a message, and God wanted him to deliver the message.

Moses insisted upon having an excuse. He didn't want to go. Instead of being eager to act as heaven's messenger and being God's errand boy, he wanted to excuse himself. The Lord humored him and gave him an interpreter; He gave him Aaron.

Now, if there is a foolish thing in the world in this case, it is to talk through an interpreter. I tried it once in Paris. The interpreter and I got up into a little box of a pulpit where there was hardly room enough for one. I said a sentence while he leaned way over to one side; then I leaned over while he repeated it in French. Can you conceive of a more foolish thing than Moses going before Pharaoh and speaking through Aaron?

This slow-of-speech man, though, became eloquent. Talk about William Gladstone's power to speak![5] When Moses was one hundred and twenty years old, he grew eloquent, as we see in Deuteronomy 32:1-4:

> *Give ear, O ye heavens, and I will speak; and hear, O earth, the words of my mouth. My doctrine shall drop as the rain, my speech shall distil as the dew, as the small rain upon the tender herb and as the showers upon the grass. Because I will invoke the name of the LORD, ascribe ye greatness unto our God. The strong One, whose work is perfect: for all His ways are right; a God of truth and without iniquity, just and upright is He.*

Moses turned out to be one of the most eloquent men the world has ever seen. If God sends men and they deliver His message, He will be with their mouth. If God has given you a message, go and give it to the people, as God has given it to you. It is a foolish thing for someone to try to be eloquent.

Make your message, and not yourself, the most prominent thing. Don't be self-conscious. Set your hearts on what God has given you to do, and do not be so foolish as to let your own difficulties or your own abilities stand in the way. It is said that people would go to hear Cicero and would come away and say, "Did you ever hear anything like it? Wasn't it sublime? Wasn't it grand?" But they would go to hear Demosthenes, and he would fire them up so much that they would want to go

5 William Gladstone (1809-1898) was a British statesman who served for more than sixty years, including four terms as the prime minister.

and fight at once. They forgot all about Demosthenes, but they were stirred by his message. That was the difference between the two men.

Next Moses said, *O my Lord, send, I pray thee, by the hand of him whom thou wilt send* (Exodus 4:13). Think what Moses would have lost if God had taken him at his word and said, "Very well, Moses. You may stay here in the desert, and I will send Aaron or Joshua or Caleb!"

Don't seek to be excused if God calls you to some service. What would the twelve disciples have lost if they had declined the call of Jesus? I have always pitied those other disciples of whom we read that they went back and walked no more with Jesus (John 6:66).

Think what Orpah missed when she returned to her people and what Ruth gained by cleaving to Naomi's God. Her story has been told these three thousand years. Her father, mother, sisters, brothers, the grave of her husband – she turned her back on them all (see Ruth 1:8-18). If Ruth could come back, she would tell us that she does not regret her choice. No. Her name shines as one of the brightest among all the women who have ever lived. The Messiah was one of her descendants.

If Moses could come back, would he tell us he was sorry that God had called him? When he stood in that glorified body on the Mount of Transfiguration with Jesus and Elijah, I don't think he regretted it.

My dear friends, God is not confined to any one messenger. We are told that He can raise up children out of stones (Matthew 3:9; Luke 3:8). Someone has said that there are three classes of people – the "wills," the "won'ts," and the "can'ts." The first accomplish everything, the second oppose everything, and the third fail in everything. If God calls you, consider it a great honor. Consider it a great privilege to have partnership with Him in anything. Do it cheerfully and gladly. Do it with all your heart, and He will bless you. Don't let false modesty, insincerity, self-interest, or any personal consideration turn you aside from the path of duty and sacrifice. If we listen for God's voice, we will hear the call. If He calls and sends us, there will be no such thing as failure, but success will accompany us all along the way. Moses had glorious success because he went forward and did what God called him to do.

Chapter 3

Naaman

God's Methods

Let us look at one who was a great and honorable man in his own country – one whom the king delighted to honor. Naaman ranked high in position as captain of the host of the king of Syria, but he was a leper, and that threw a cloud over his whole life. As Bishop Hall quaintly put it, the lowest slave in Syria would not have changed skins with him.

You cannot have a better type of a sinner than Naaman was. I don't care who or what he is or what position he holds – all people alike have sinned. *All have sinned and are made destitute of the glory of God* (Romans 3:23). All have to bear the same burden of death, *for the wages of sin is death* (Romans 6:23). All people must stand in judgment before God. What a gloom that throws over our whole life!

But he was a leper (2 Kings 5:1). There was no physician in Syria who could help him. None of the eminent doctors in Damascus could do him any good. If he was to be cured of the leprosy, the power would have to come from on high. It had to be someone unknown to Naaman, for he did not know God.

But they had something else in Syria – they had one of God's children there. She was a little girl, a simple captive maid, who waited on Mrs. Naaman. Naaman knew nothing about this little Israelite, even though she was one of his household.

I can imagine that one day, as she was waiting on the general's wife, she noticed Naaman's wife weeping. The heart of the little maid was breaking because of the dark cloud that rested over the home, so she told her mistress that there was a prophet in her country who could cure her master of his leprosy. She said, *If my lord would ask the prophet that is in Samaria, he would remove his leprosy* (2 Kings 5:3).

Now there is faith for you! She boasted of God that He would do more for the heathen Naaman than He had done for any in Israel, and God honored her faith.

Naaman's wife might have said to the young maid, "What? A prophet in Israel who can cure leprosy?"

"Yes."

"Do you know of anyone who was ever cured?

"No."

"Well, then, what makes you think there is a prophet who can cure leprosy?"

"Oh, that is nothing compared to what Elisha can do. A little boy lived near us who died, and Elisha raised him to life. He has done many wonderful things."

She must have had a reputation for truthfulness,

for if she hadn't, her testimony would not have been taken seriously. Someone told the general, and he made it known to the king. Naaman was highly respected by the king, for he had recently won a great victory. He stood near the throne. So the king said, "You had better go down to Samaria and see if this is true. I will give you letters of introduction to the king of Israel."

Yes, he would give Naaman letters of introduction to the king. That's how people work. The thought was that if anybody could help him, it would be the king, and the king had power both with God and man. Oh, my friends, it is much better to know a man who knows God. A man acquainted with God has more power than any earthly ruler. Gold can't do everything.

Away went Naaman down to Samaria with his kingly introduction. What a stir it must have made when the commander of the Syrian army drove up! Naaman had brought with him much gold and silver. That is man's idea again. He was going to pay for a great doctor, and he took about five hundred thousand dollars to pay for the doctor's bill.

Many men would willingly pay that much money if they could buy the favor of God and get rid of the curse of sin. Yes, if money could do it, many would buy salvation; but thank God that salvation is not for sale. We must buy it at God's price, and that is *without money and without price* (Isaiah 55:1). Naaman found that out.

My dear friends, did you ever ask yourselves which is worse – the leprosy of sin or the leprosy of the body? For my own part, I would a thousand times rather have the leprosy of the body eating into my eyes and feet and arms. I would rather be loathsome in the sight of my fellow men than die with the leprosy of sin in my soul and be banished from God forever. The leprosy of the body is bad, but the leprosy of sin is incalculably worse. It has cast angels out of heaven. It has ruined the best and strongest men who ever lived in the world. Oh, how it has pulled people down! The leprosy of the body could not do that.

There is one thing that I particularly like about Naaman, and that is his earnestness of purpose. He was thoroughly intense and sincere. He was quite willing to go one hundred and fifty miles and take the advice of this little maid. Many people say, "Oh, I don't like such and such a minister; I would like to know where he comes from and what he has done, and whether any bishop has laid his hands on his head."

My dear friends, never mind the minister; it is the message you need. If someone were to send me a message, and the news was important, I wouldn't stop to ask about the messenger who brought it. I would want to read the news. I would look at the message and not at the one who brought it.

So it is with God's message. The good news is everything, but the minister is nothing. The Syrians looked down with contempt on the Israelites, yet this great man was willing to take the good news at the hands of this little maiden and listen to the words that fell from her lips.

If I got lost in New York City, I would be willing to ask anybody which way to go, even if it were only a shoe-shine boy. In fact, a boy's word in such a case is often better than a man's word. It is the way to where I'm going that I want – not the person who directs me.

There was one drawback in Naaman's case. Though he was willing to take the advice of the little girl, he was not willing to take the remedy. The stumbling block of pride stood in his way. The remedy the prophet offered him was a terrible blow to his pride. I have no doubt he expected a grand reception from the king of Israel to whom he brought letters of introduction. He had been victorious on many battlefields and held a high rank in the army. Perhaps we could call him Major General Naaman of Syria, or he might have been even higher in rank than that.

Bringing with him kingly credentials, he no doubt expected a distinguished reception; but instead of the king rushing out to meet him, when he heard of Naaman's arrival and purpose, he simply tore his clothes and asked, *Am I God, to kill and to give life, that this man sends unto me to remove the leprosy of this man? Therefore now consider and see how he seeks a quarrel against me* (2 Kings 5:7).

Elisha heard of the king's trouble and sent him a message saying, *Why hast thou rent thy clothes? Let him come now to me, and he shall know that there is a prophet in Israel* (2 Kings 5:8).

I can imagine Naaman's pride reasoning like this: "Surely the prophet will feel very exalted and flattered that I, the great Syrian general, would come and call upon him." So, probably full of those proud thoughts, he drove up to the prophet's humble dwelling with his chariot and his splendid attire. Yes, Naaman drove up in grand style to the prophet's abode, and when nobody seemed to be coming out to greet him, he sent in his message: "Tell the prophet that Major General Naaman of Syria has arrived and wishes to see him."

Elisha took it very calmly. He did not come out to see Naaman, but as soon as he heard of Naaman's errand, he sent his servant to tell him to dip seven times in the Jordan River, and he would be clean.

That was a terrible blow to Naaman's pride. I can imagine he might have said to his servant, "What did you say? Did I understand you correctly? Dip seven times in the Jordan! Why, we call the Jordan River a ditch in our country."

But the only answer he got was that the prophet says, *Go and wash in the Jordan seven times, and thy flesh shall be restored, and thou shalt be clean* (2 Kings 5:10).

I can imagine Naaman's indignation as he asks, *Are not Abana and Pharpar, rivers of Damascus, better than all the waters of Israel? May I not wash in them and be clean?* (2 Kings 5:12). He might have thought, "Haven't I bathed myself hundreds of times, and has it helped me? Can water wash away leprosy?" So he turned and went away in a rage.

It isn't a bad sign when a man gets mad if you tell him the truth. Some people are afraid of getting other people mad. I have known wives afraid to talk to their husbands, afraid of getting them mad. I have known mothers who were afraid to talk to their sons because they were afraid they would get mad.

Don't be afraid of making them mad, if the truth is what makes them mad. If our foolishness makes them mad, then we have reason to mourn over it. If the truth makes someone angry, God sent it, and it is much better to have someone get angry than it is to have him go to sleep. I think the trouble with many people today is that they are sound asleep. It is much better to awaken them, even if they do wake up mad.

The fact was that the Jordan never had any great reputation as a river. It flowed into the Dead Sea, and that sea never had a harbor to it. Its banks were not half as beautiful as those of the rivers of Damascus. Damascus was one of the most beautiful cities in the world.

Naaman turned away in a rage. "Ah," he said, "here am I, a great conqueror, a successful general on the battlefield, holding the very highest rank in the army, and yet this prophet does not even come out to meet me. He simply sends a message. *I thought, He will surely come out to me and stand and call on the name of the LORD, his God, and strike his hand over the place and remove the leprosy* (2 Kings 5:11).

There it is. I hardly ever knew a man who, when talked to about his sins, didn't say, "Yes, but *I thought* so and so."

"Mr. Moody," they say, "I will tell you what *I think;* I will tell you *my opinion.*"

In the fifty-fifth chapter of Isaiah, God says, *For my thoughts are not as your thoughts, neither are your ways as my ways, saith the LORD* (Isaiah 55:8). So it was with Naaman. In the first place, he thought a good big doctor's fee would take care of it and settle everything up. Besides that, he also thought that going to the king with his letters of introduction would do it. Yes, those were Naaman's first thoughts. *I thought.* Exactly so. He turned away in rage and disappointment.

He thought the prophet would have come out to him very humble and obedient and ask him to do some great thing. Instead of that, Elisha, who was perhaps busy writing, did not even come to the door or the window. He merely sent out the message, *Go and wash in the Jordan seven times* (2 Kings 5:10), and away went Naaman, saying, *I thought, I thought, I thought.*

I have heard that story so often that I am tired of it. Give it up and take God's words, God's thoughts, and God's ways. I never yet knew a man who was converted in the time and manner he expected to be. I have heard people say, "Well, if I am ever converted, it won't be in a Methodist church; you won't catch me there." I never knew anyone say that, but if converted at all, it was in a Methodist church.

In Scotland, a man – an employer – was converted at one of our meetings. He was very concerned that all his employees should be reached, and he sent them one by one to the meetings. There was one man, though, who wouldn't go. We are all more or less troubled with stubbornness, and the moment this man found out that his employer wanted him to go to the meetings, he made up his mind he wouldn't go. If he was going to be converted, he said, he was going to be converted by some ordained minister. He was not going to any meeting that was conducted by Americans who were not ordained. He believed in conversion, but he was going to be converted the regular way.

He believed in the regular Presbyterian Church of Scotland, and that was the place for him to be converted. The employer tried every way he could to get him to attend the meetings, but he wouldn't go.

After we left that town and went up to Inverness, the employer had some business up there, and he sent this employee to take care of that business, hoping that he would attend some of our meetings.

One night as I was preaching on the banks of a river, I happened to take this for my text: "I thought; I thought." I was trying to address people's thoughts and show the difference between their thoughts and God's thoughts. This man happened to be walking along the banks of the river. He saw a large crowd and heard someone talking. He wondered what that man was talking about. He didn't know who was there, so he approached the crowd and listened. He heard the sermon and became convicted and converted right there. Then he inquired who the preacher was, and he found out it was the very man he said he would not listen to – the man he disliked. The very man he had been talking against was the very man God used to convert him.

While Naaman was thus wavering in his mind and thinking about what to do, one of his servants drew near and made a very sensible remark: *My father, if the prophet had bid thee do some great thing, would thou not have done it? How much rather then, when he saith to thee, Wash, and be clean?* (2 Kings 5:13).

There is a great deal of truth in that. If Elisha had told him to go back to Syria on his hands and knees, one hundred and fifty miles, he would have done it and thought it was all right. If he had told him to go into some cave and stay there a year or two, he would have done it and thought it was all right. If he had told him it was necessary to have some surgery performed along with much accompanying pain, that would have suited him.

People like to have something to do about their salvation. They don't like to give up the idea that they can't do anything and that God must do it all. If you tell them to take bitter herbs every morning and every night for the next five years, they think that's all right. If Elisha had told Naaman to do that, he would have done it; but to tell him merely to dip in the Jordan River seven times seemed absurd. But this servant suggested to him that he had better go down to the Jordan and try the remedy, as it was a very simple one.

Now, don't you see yourselves there? How many people wait for some great thing? They wait for some sudden feeling to come gliding over them, or they wait for some shock to come upon them. That is not what the Lord wants. There is a man whom I have talked to about his soul for a number of years, and the last time I talked with him, he said, "Well, the thing hasn't struck me yet."

I said, "What?"

"Well," he said, "the thing hasn't struck me yet."

"Struck you? What do you mean?"

"Well," he said, "I go to church, and I hear you preach, and I hear other men preach, but the thing hasn't struck me yet. It strikes some people, but it hasn't struck me yet."

That was all that I could get out of him. Many people reason in that way. They have heard some young converts tell how light dawned upon them like the flash of a meteor, or how they experienced a new sensation, so they are waiting for something like that. But you can't find any place in Scripture where you are told to wait for anything of the kind. You are just to obey what God tells you to do and let your feelings take care of themselves.

I can't control my feelings. I can't make myself feel good or bad when I want to, but I can obey God. God gives me the power. He doesn't command me to do something without giving me the power to do it. With the command comes the power.

Naaman could do what the prophet told him. He could go down to the Jordan and dip seven times, and that is what the Lord had for him to do. If we are going to get into the kingdom of God, then right at the threshold of that kingdom we have to learn this doctrine of obedience – to do whatever He tells us.

I can imagine Naaman still reluctant to believe it, saying, "If there is such cleansing power in the waters of Jordan, why wouldn't every leper in Israel go down and dip in them and be healed?"

"Well," the servant might have urged, "now that you have come a hundred and fifty miles, don't you think you should do what he told you? After all, you can at least try it. He sent word distinctly, my lord, that your flesh will again become like that of a little child."

Naaman in time accepted his servant's recommendation. His anger was cooling down, and he was over the first rush of his indignation. He said, "Well, I might as well try it."

That was the starting point of his faith, although he still thought it was a foolish idea to dip in the Jordan River, and he could not bring himself to believe that he would be healed by following the prophet's instructions. At last, however, Naaman's will was conquered, and he surrendered.

When General Grant besieged a town that was a stronghold of the Southern Confederacy, some of the officers sent word that they would leave the city if he would let them go with their men. General Grant replied, "No, nothing but an unconditional surrender!"

Then they sent word that they would go if he would let them take their flag with them. But the answer was "No – an unconditional surrender." At last General Grant and his men broke down the walls and entered the city, and then the enemy made a complete and unconditional surrender.

That is how it was with Naaman; he got to the point where he was willing to obey, and God prefers obedience over sacrifice. The Bible tells us that *To hear is better than sacrifice* (1 Samuel 15:22). God wants obedience, and Naaman had to learn this lesson. There was probably no virtue in going down to the Jordan, other than in obeying the voice of God. Naaman had to obey the word, and in the very act of obedience, he was blessed.

Look at those ten New Testament lepers who came

to Christ. He said to them, *Go show yourselves unto the priests* (Luke 17:14).

"Well," they might have said, "what good is that going to do us? Here we are all full of leprosy, and if we go and show ourselves to the priests, they will order us back again into exile. That is not going to help us."

But those ten men started off and did just what the Lord Jesus Christ told them to do, and in the very act of doing it, they were blessed; their leprosy left them.

Jesus said to the man who had the palsy, whose friends brought him upon a bed to Jesus, *Take up thy bed, and walk* (John 5:8).

The man could have said, "Lord, I have been trying for years to take up that bed, but I can't. I don't have the power. I have been shaking with the palsy for the last ten years. Do you think that I would have been brought here and let down through the roof if I could have rolled up that bed? I don't have the power." But when the Lord commanded him, He gave him the power. Power came with the command, and that man stood up, rolled up his bed, and started for home. He was blessed in the very act of obedience. My friends, if you want God to bless you, obey Him. Do whatever He calls upon you to do, and then see if He will not bless you.

Christ went to the synagogue one day. The Pharisees wanted to get Him to do something to break the law of Moses so they could condemn Him to death. There was a man there with a withered hand. The Pharisees asked Jesus if it was lawful to heal on the Sabbath, to see if He would heal on that day. Jesus said to the man, *Stretch forth thine hand* (Matthew 12:13).

The man could have said, "Lord, that is a very strange command. I don't have the power. That hand has been withered for twenty years. I haven't stretched it out for the last twenty years, and you say, 'Stretch it out.'"

But when Jesus told him to do it, He also gave him the power, and out went that old withered hand; and before it came out straight, right in the act of stretching, the hand was made whole. He was blessed in the very act of obedience.

Naaman had to be taught the lesson that he had to obey, so he finally went down to the Jordan as he was told to do. If you will do what the Lord tells you, the Lord will bless you as He did Naaman.

You may ask, "What does He tell me?"

He says, *Believe on the Lord Jesus Christ, and thou shalt be saved* (Acts 16:31).

The word of God to Naaman was to go and wash. The word of God to every soul out of Christ is to believe on His Son. *Verily, verily, I say unto you, he that hears my word and believes him that sent Me has eternal life and shall not come into judgment but has passed from death unto life* (John 5:24). If you believe with all your heart on the Lord Jesus Christ, God will never bring you to judgment for sin; that is all passed – that is all gone. Take Him at His word; believe Him. Believe what He says, and you will enter into life eternal. *He came unto his own, and his own received Him not* (John 1:11). Notice that you are to take *Him* – not a dogma, not a creed, not a myth, but a person.

He came unto His own, and his own received him not. But as many as received him, to them gave he power to become sons of God (John 1:11-12). That is the way you get the power.

Naaman went down to the river and took the first dip. I can imagine him looking at himself when he came up and saying to his servant, "There! There I am – no better than I was when I went in! If one-seventh of the leprosy was gone, I would be content."

Maybe the servant said, "The man of God told you to dip seven times. Do as he told you. There is no partial obedience to God's word."

Well, down he went a second time, and he came up puffing and blowing, as much a leper as ever, but he went down again and again – the third, fourth, fifth, and sixth time with the same result, as much a leper as ever. Some of the people standing on the banks of the river might have said, as they certainly would in our day, "That man has gone clear out of his mind!"

When he came up the sixth time, he looked at himself and said, "No better! What a fool I have made of myself! How they will all laugh at me! I wouldn't want the generals and aristocracy of Damascus to know that I have been dipping in the Jordan for all the world. However, since I have gone so far, I'll make the seventh plunge."

He had not altogether lost faith; down he went the seventh time and came up again. He looked at himself and shouted aloud for joy. "I am well! My leprosy is all gone, all gone! My flesh is restored like that of a little child!" If one speck of leprosy had remained, it would have been a reflection on God.

If we could have asked Naaman how he felt, he

might have said, "How do I feel? This is the happiest day of my life! I thought that day when I won a great victory upon the battlefield was the most joyful day of my life. I thought I would never be so happy again, but that wasn't anything compared with this hour. My leprosy is all gone. I am whole, I am cleansed!"

Naaman first lost his temper, then he lost his pride, and then he lost his leprosy. That is generally the order in which proud, rebellious sinners are converted.

He came up out of the Jordan, put on his clothes, and went back to see the prophet. He was mad with Elisha in the beginning, but when he was cleansed, his anger was all gone, too. Naaman wanted to pay Elisha. Naaman wanted to give money for his cure. People want to do the same thing today. It would have spoiled the story of grace if the prophet had taken anything. The Lord doesn't charge anything to save you. Salvation is *without money and without price* (Isaiah 55:1). The prophet Elisha refused to take anything, and I can imagine no one rejoiced more than he did.

Naaman headed back to Damascus a very different man than he was when he had left it. The dark cloud was gone from his mind; he was no longer a leper in fear of dying from a loathsome disease. He lost the leprosy in the Jordan when he did what the man of God told him to do.

If you obey the voice of God, even at this very moment, the burden of your sins will fall from you, and you will be cleansed. It is all done through faith and obedience.

Let us see what Naaman's faith led him to believe. *And*

he returned to the man of God, he and all his company, and came and stood before him, and he said, Behold, now I know that there is no God in all the earth, but in Israel. Now therefore, I pray thee, take a blessing from thy slave (2 Kings 5:15).

Particularly pay attention to the words *I know*. There is no hesitation about it and no qualifying the expression. Naaman doesn't say, "I think." He says, "*I know* there is a God who has power to cleanse the leprosy."

Here is another thought: Naaman left only one thing in Samaria, and that was his leprosy. The only thing God wants you to leave with Him is your sin, yet it is the only thing you seem not to care about giving up.

"Oh," you say, "I love leprosy. It is so delightful, I can't give it up. I know God wants it so that He can make me clean, but I can't give it up." What downright craziness it is for you to love leprosy, and yet that is your condition.

"Well," says someone, "I don't believe in sudden conversions." Don't you? How long did it take Naaman to be cured? The seventh time he went down, away went the leprosy. Read the great conversions recorded in the Bible: Saul of Tarsus, Zacchaeus, and a host of others. How long did it take the Lord to transform them? They were changed in a minute. We are born in iniquity, shaped in it, dead in trespasses and sins; but when spiritual life comes, it comes in a moment, and we are free from both sin and death.

When Naaman got home, I am sure there was no little commotion in his house. I can see his wife, Mrs. Naaman, who had probably been watching and looking out of the window for him with a great burden on her heart. "Well, husband, how is it?" she asked. I can see the tears running down his cheeks as he answered, "Thank God, I am well." They embrace each other and pour out mutual expressions of joy and gladness. The servants are just as glad as their master and mistress, as they had been waiting eagerly for the news. There was never a happier household than Naaman's was after he was rid of the leprosy.

And so, my friends, it will be the same with your households when you get rid of the leprosy of sin today. Not only will there be joy in your hearts and homes, but there will also be joy among the saints in heaven.

Once, as I was walking down the street, I heard some people laughing and talking loudly. One of them said, "Well, there will be no difference; it will be all the same a hundred years from now."

The thought flashed across my mind, "Will there be no difference? Where will you be a hundred years from now?"

Young man, ask yourself this question: "Where will I be?" Some of you who are getting on in years may be in eternity ten years from now. Where will you be – on the left or the right hand of God? I cannot answer for you, but I must answer for myself. I ask you, "Where will you spend eternity? Where will you be a hundred years from now?"

I once heard of a man who went to England from mainland Europe and brought letters with him from the emperor addressed to prominent physicians. The letters said, "This man is a personal friend of mine, and we are afraid he is going to lose his mental capabilities. Do all you can for him."

The doctor asked him if he had lost any dear friend in his own country, or any position of importance, or what it was that was weighing on his mind. The young man said, "No, but my father and grandfather and myself were brought up as unbelievers, and for the last two or three years this thought has been haunting me: *Where will I spend eternity?* And the thought of it follows me day and night."

The doctor said, "You have come to the wrong physician, but I will tell you of one who can cure you." He told him about Christ and read to him the fifty-third chapter of Isaiah. *He was wounded for our rebellions; he was bruised for our iniquities; the chastisement of our peace was upon him; and by his stripes healing was provided for us* (Isaiah 53:5).

The young man asked, "Doctor, do you believe that?"

The doctor told him he did, and he prayed and wrestled with the young man. At last, the clear light of Calvary shone on his soul. At last, he had settled the question in his own mind of where he would spend eternity. I ask you, sinner, to settle it now. It is for you to decide. Will it be with the saints, martyrs, and prophets, or in the dark caverns of hell, surrounded by misery and darkness forever? Make haste to be wise, for *how shall we escape, if we belittle such great saving health?* (Hebrews 2:3).

At our church in Chicago, as I was closing the meeting one day, a young soldier got up and begged the people to decide for Christ at once. He said he had just come from a dark scene. A friend of his who had enlisted with him had a father who was always urging him to become a Christian. The friend always replied that he would when the war was over.

Well, he was wounded and was put into the hospital, but he got worse, and was gradually sinking near to death. One day, a few hours before he died, a letter came from his sister, but he was too weak to read it. Oh, it was such an earnest letter! The young soldier read it to him, but the dying man did not seem to understand it, as he was so weak, until he came to the last sentence, which said, "Oh, my dear brother, when you get this letter, will you not accept your sister's Savior?"

The dying man sprang up from his cot and said, "What do you say? What do you say?" and then, falling back on his pillow, he feebly exclaimed, "It is too late! It is too late!"

My dear friends, thank God it is not too late for you today. The Master is still calling you. Let every one of us, young and old, rich and poor, come to Christ at once, and He will put all our sins away. Don't wait any longer for feelings, but obey at once. You can believe, you can trust, you can lay hold on eternal life, if you will. Will you not do it now?

Chapter 4
Nehemiah

Uncompromising Vision

I want to call your attention now to the prophet Nehemiah. We can find some help from that distinguished man who accomplished a great work. He was one of the last of the prophets, supposedly contemporary with Malachi. His book might have been one of the last of the Old Testament books written. He may have known Daniel, for he was a young man in the declining years of that very eminent and godly statesman. We are sure of one thing: Nehemiah was a man of sterling worth. Although he was brought up in the Persian court among idolaters, he had a character that has remained untarnished all these centuries.

Notice his prayer in which he made confession of Israel's apostasy from God (Nehemiah 1:4-11). There may be some confessions we need to make in order to be brought into close fellowship with God. I have no doubt that many Christians hunger and thirst for a personal blessing and have a great desire to grow closer to God. If that is the desire of your heart, you must keep in mind that if there is some obstacle that you can remove, you will not get a blessing until you remove it. We must cooperate with God.

If there is any sin in my heart that I am not willing to give up, then I do not need to pray. You can take a bottle, cork it up tight, and put it under Niagara Falls, and not a drop of that mighty volume of water will get into the bottle. If there is any sin in my heart that I am not willing to give up, I do not need to expect a blessing. The people who have had power with God in prayer have always begun by confessing their sins.

Consider the prayers of Jeremiah and Daniel. Jeremiah cried to the Lord: *We acknowledge, O LORD, our wickedness, and the iniquity of our fathers; for we have sinned against thee* (Jeremiah 14:20). Jeremiah confessed the sins of the people as if he had been one of the guilty ones.

See how David confessed his sins and what power he had with God (see Psalm 32 and Psalm 51). Daniel confessed his sin, when there isn't a single sin recorded against him; but he confessed his sin and the sins of the people. Notice how Daniel confessed his sins and the sins of the people and what power he had with God.

> *And I prayed unto the LORD my God and made my confession and said, Now O Lord, thou great God who is worthy to be feared, who keeps the covenant and the mercy with those that love thee and keep thy*

commandments; we have sinned, we have committed iniquity, we have done wickedly, and we have been rebels and we have departed from thy commandments and from thy judgments. We have not hearkened unto thy slaves the prophets, who spoke in thy name to our kings and to our princes, to our fathers, and to all the people of the land. . . . O Lord, according to all thy righteousness, let thine anger and thy fury be turned away from thy city Jerusalem, thy holy mountain: because for our sins and for the iniquities of our fathers, Jerusalem and all thy people is given in reproach to all that are about us.

Now therefore, O our God, hear the prayer of thy slave and his supplications and cause thy face to shine upon thy sanctuary that is made desolate, by the Lord. O my God, incline thine ear and hear; open thine eyes, and behold our desolations, and the city which is called by thy name: for we do not present our supplications before thee confiding in our righteousnesses, but in thy many mercies. O Lord, hear; O Lord, forgive; O Lord, hearken and do; defer not, for thine own sake, O my God: for thy city and thy people are called by thy name.

And whiles I was speaking and praying, and confessing my sin and the sin of my people Israel and presenting my supplication before the LORD my God for the holy mountain of

> *my God; I was even yet speaking in prayers and that man Gabriel, whom I had seen in the vision at the beginning, flying swiftly, touched me about the time of the evening sacrifice.*
> (Daniel 9:4-6, 16-21)

It is a good thing for us to begin as Nehemiah did – with prayer. It seems that some men had come from his country to the Persian court, perhaps to see the king on business. Nehemiah, who was in high favor with the king, met them, and learning that they had come from Jerusalem, he inquired about his country (Nehemiah 1:1-3). He not only loved his God, but he loved his country.

I like to see a patriotic man. Nehemiah inquired about his people and about the city, Jerusalem, that was very near to his heart. He had never seen the city. He had no relations back there in Jerusalem that he knew of. Nehemiah was not a Jewish prince, although it is supposed he had royal blood in his veins. He was born in captivity. It was about one hundred years after Jerusalem had been taken that he appeared on the scene. He was in the court of Artaxerxes as a cupbearer to the king, and he held a high position; yet he longed to hear from his native land.

When these men told him the condition of the city, that the people were in great need and distress and degradation, that the walls of the city were still down and the gates had been burned and not yet restored – Nehemiah's patriotic heart began to burn. We are told he fasted and prayed and wept; not only did he pray for one week or one month, but he kept on praying. He prayed *day and night* (Nehemiah 1:6).

Having many duties to perform, of course he was not always on his knees, but in his heart he was always before the throne of grace. It was not hard for him to understand and obey the precept, *Pray without ceasing* (1 Thessalonians 5:17). He began the work in prayer, continued in prayer, and the last recorded words of Nehemiah are a prayer.

Those men had arrived at that court in November or December, but Nehemiah prayed until March or April before he spoke to the king (Nehemiah 1:1; 2:1). If a blessing doesn't come tonight, pray harder tomorrow, and if it doesn't come tomorrow, pray harder; then if it doesn't come, keep right on praying; you will not be disappointed. God in heaven will hear your prayers, and He will answer them. He has never failed to do so, if one has been honest in his petitions and honest in his confessions. Let faith produce patience. According to Augustine, God is never in a hurry, because He has all eternity to work.

The first chapter of Nehemiah contains the prayer of this wonderful man. His prayer has been on record all these years and has been a great help to many people:

> *I beseech thee, O LORD God of heavens, strong, great and terrible, who keeps covenant and mercy for those that love thee and observe thy commandments; let thine ear now be attentive and thine eyes open, that thou may hear the prayer of thy slave, which I pray*

before thee now, day and night, for the sons of Israel, thy slaves, and I confess the sins of the sons of Israel, with which we have sinned against thee; both I and my father's house have sinned.

We have dealt very corruptly against thee and have not kept the commandments nor the statutes nor the judgments, which thou didst command thy slave Moses. Remember, I beseech thee, the word that thou didst command thy slave Moses, saying, If ye transgress, I will scatter you abroad among the peoples; but if ye turn unto me and keep my commandments and do them; though there were of you cast out unto the uttermost part of the heavens, yet will I gather them from there and will bring them unto the place that I have chosen to cause my name to dwell there. Now these are thy slaves and thy people, whom thou hast ransomed with thy great power and with thy strong hand.

O Lord, I beseech thee, let now thine ear be attentive to the prayer of thy slave and to the prayer of thy slaves who desire to fear thy name; and prosper, I pray thee, thy slave this day, and grant him grace before this man. (Nehemiah 1:5-11)

When he began to pray, I do not think that he thought he was to be the instrument in God's hand for building the walls of Jerusalem. But when a man gets into sympathy and harmony with God, God prepares him for the work He has for him. No doubt he thought the Persian king might send one of his great warriors to accomplish the work with a great army of men, but after he had prayed for months, he may have thought, "Why shouldn't I go to Jerusalem myself and build those walls?" Prayer for the work will soon arouse your own sympathy and effort.

It meant a lot for Nehemiah to give up the palace of Shushan and his high office and to identify himself with the despised and captive Jews. He was among the highest in the whole realm. Not only that, but he was a man of wealth, lived in ease and luxury, and had great influence at the court. For him to go to Jerusalem and lose his position was like Moses turning his back on the palace of Pharaoh and identifying himself with the Hebrew slaves; yet we might never have heard of either of them if they had not done this. They humbled themselves to conquer, and when you humble yourself, God will bless you.

Plato, Socrates, and other Greek philosophers lived in the same century as Nehemiah. How few have heard of them and read their words compared with the millions who have heard and read of Nehemiah during the last two thousand years. If we are to be blessed in this world, we must be willing to take any position into which God puts us.

So, after Nehemiah had prayed a while, he began to pray that God would send him and that he might be the man to rebuild the walls of Jerusalem. After Nehemiah had been praying for a while, he was in the banqueting hall one day, and the king noticed that his countenance was sad. We might not have called the face sad, but much prayer and fasting changes the very countenance of a person. I know some godly men and women who seem to have the stamp of heaven on them. The king noticed a strange look about this cupbearer, and he questioned him. Then the thought came to Nehemiah that he would tell the king what caused his sorrow – how his own nation was degraded and how his heart was breaking for his own country. After he had told the king, the king asked, "What is your request?"

Now, some people tell us they don't have time to pray, but I say that if anyone has God's work lying deep in his heart, he will have time to pray. Nehemiah shot up a prayer to heaven right there in the king's dining hall that the Lord would help him make his request in the right way. I have little doubt that he first looked beyond Artaxerxes to the King of Kings. We don't need to make long prayers. Someone who prays much in private will make short prayers in public.

The Lord told Nehemiah what to ask for – that he might be sent to his own country, that some men might go with him, and that the king would give him letters to the governors through whose provinces he would pass, so that he might have a profitable journey and be able to rebuild the walls of his city. God had been preparing the king, for the king at once granted the request, and before long, Nehemiah was on his way to Jerusalem.

When he reached the city, he didn't send a lot of men to go before him blowing trumpets and announcing that the cupbearer of the great Persian king, the converted cupbearer, had arrived from the Persian court and was ready to build the walls of Jerusalem. Some people always talk about what they are going to do. Let the work speak for itself. You don't need to blow any horns; go and do the work, and it will advertise itself. Nehemiah didn't have any newspapers writing about him or any billboards. However, there was no little commotion. No doubt, everyone in town was talking about it, saying that a very important person had arrived from the Persian court; but he was there three days and three nights without telling anyone why he had come.

One night he went out to survey the city. He tried to ride around the walls of Jerusalem, but he couldn't, so he walked around. It was a difficult task that he had before him, but he was not discouraged. That is what makes character. People who can go into a hard field and succeed are the people we need. Many people look for easy places, but the world will never hear of them. We need people who look for difficult places, who are willing to go into the darkest corners of the earth and make those dark places bloom like gardens. They can do it if the Lord is with them.

Everything looked dark before Nehemiah. The walls were broken down. There was not a man of influence or a man of culture or wealth among the people. The nations all around were looking down on these weak, feeble Jews. So it is in many churches today. The walls are down and people say it is no use; their hands drop down by their side. Everything seemed against Nehemiah, but he was a man who had the fire of God in his soul. He had come to build the walls of Jerusalem.

If we could have seen into his head, we would have found *Jerusalem* stamped on his brain. If we could have looked into his heart, we would have found *Jerusalem* there. He was a fanatic. He was terribly in earnest. He was an enthusiast. I like to see a man take up a cause and say, "I will do it. I live for this thing. This one thing I am determined to do." We spread ourselves so thin by trying to do so many things, that the world never hears of us.

After Nehemiah had been in the city three days and nights, he called the elders of Israel together and told them why he had come. God had been preparing them, for the moment he told them they said, *Let us rise up and build* (Nehemiah 2:18).

There has not been a work undertaken for God since Adam fell that has not met with opposition. If Satan allows us to work unhindered, it is because our work is of no consequence. The first thing we read after the decision had been made to rebuild the walls is: *When Sanballat, the Horonite, and Tobiah, the slave, the Ammonite, and Geshem, the Arabian, heard it, they laughed us to scorn and despised us and said, What is this thing that ye do? Will ye rebel against the king?* (Nehemiah 2:19).

These men were very indignant. They didn't care for the well-being of Jerusalem. Who were they? They were a mixed multitude who had *no portion nor righteousness, nor memorial in Jerusalem* (Nehemiah 2:20). They didn't like to see the restoration of the ruins, just as people today do not like to see the cause of Christ prosper. The offence of the cross has not ceased.

It doesn't take long to build the walls of a city if you can just get all the people at it. If the Christians of this country would rise up, we could evangelize America in twelve months. All the Jews had a hand in repairing the walls of Jerusalem. Each person – priest and merchant, goldsmith and apothecary, and even the women – built over against their own house. The men of Jericho and other cities came to help. The walls began to rise.

This stirred up Nehemiah's enemies, and they began to ridicule. Ridicule is a mighty weapon. *What are these feeble Jews doing?* asked Sanballat. *Is this to be permitted them? Will they sacrifice? Will they finish on time? Will they resurrect the stones out of the heaps of the rubbish which were burned?* (Nehemiah 4:2). *Even that which they build, if a fox were to go up it, he would break down their stone wall*, said Tobiah the Ammonite (Nehemiah 4:3).

Nehemiah was wise. He paid no attention to them. He just looked to God for grace and comfort: *Hear, O our God; for we are despised; and turn their reproach upon their own head, and give them for a prey in the land of their captivity. And do not cover their iniquity, nor let their sin be blotted out from before thee, for they have become angry against the builders* (Nehemiah 4:4-5).

Young man, if you wish to be successful in this world, pay no attention to Sanballat or Tobiah. Don't be kept out of the kingdom of God or out of active Christian work by the scorn and laughter and ridicule of your godless neighbors and companions.

Next, these enemies conspired to come and fight against Jerusalem. Nehemiah was warned, so he took steps to guard against them. Half of the people were on watch, and the other half held a sword in one hand and a trowel in the other. There was no eight-hour workday then; they were on duty from the rising of the morning sun until the stars appeared. They did not take off their clothes except to wash them. Imagine this man who had come from the Persian court with all its luxury, living and sleeping in his clothes for fifty-two days! But he was in earnest. Ah, that is what we need! We need people who will set themselves to do one thing and keep at it day and night.

All the people were instructed to lodge within the city so they would always be on hand to work and fight. If only we could get all who belong inside the church to come in and do their share. "Happy is the church," someone says, "whose workers are well-skilled in the use of the Scripture, so that while strenuously building the gospel wall, they can fight if an occasion requires it." We all ought to be ready to use the Sword of the Spirit.

After a while, some men wrote a friendly letter and wanted Nehemiah to go down on the plain of Ono and have a friendly discussion (Nehemiah 6:1-7). It is a masterpiece of the devil to get people into friendly discussions. Nehemiah did not have a typewriter or a printed form letter in those days, but he always sent back the same reply: *I am doing a great work so that I cannot come down* (Nehemiah 6:3).

How many churches have turned aside for years to discuss "questions of the day" and have neglected the salvation of the world because they had to go down to the "plain of Ono" and have a friendly discussion. Nehemiah had a good policy: *I am doing a great work so that I cannot come down.* If God has sent you to build the walls of Jerusalem, you go and do it.

They sent him another letter, and again he sent word back: *I am doing a great work so that I cannot come down.* He did not believe in "coming down." They sent him another letter, and he sent back the same word. They sent him a fourth letter with the same result. They wanted to kill him on the way, but they could not get him to come down.

I have seen many Christian men on the plain of Ono – men who were doing a splendid work but had been distracted and turned aside. Think how much work has been neglected by temperance advocates in this country because they have gone into politics or began discussing other issues. How many times has the Young Men's Christian Association been side-tracked by discussing some other subject instead of holding Christ up before a lost world? If the church would only continue building the walls of Jerusalem, the walls would soon be built. It is a shrewd devil that we have to contend with. Do you know it? If he can get the church to stop its work to discuss these questions, he has accomplished his desire.

Nehemiah's enemies wrote him one more letter, an open letter, in which they wrote that they were going to report him to the king because they heard that he was going to set up a kingdom in opposition to the

Persians. Treason has an ugly sound, but Nehemiah committed himself to the Lord and went on building.

Then his enemies hired a prophet – one of his friends. A hundred enemies outside are not half as hard to deal with as one inside – a false friend. When the devil gets possession of a child of God, that person will do the work better than the devil himself. Temptations are never so dangerous as when they come to us in a religious appearance. Tobiah and Sanballat bought up one of the prophets and hired him to try to persuade Nehemiah to go into the temple that they might put him to death there. He said, "Nehemiah, there is a plan to kill you. Come into the temple. Let's go in and stay for the night."

Nehemiah was not deceived, and he said, *Should such a man as I flee? And who is there as I who could go into the temple and live? I will not go in* (Nehemiah 6:11). After he had refused the invitation, he realized that this man was a false prophet; so by standing his ground, he succeeded in building the walls of Jerusalem in fifty-two days. Then the gates were set up and the work was finished.

During all these centuries, this story has been told. If Nehemiah had remained at the Persian court, he might have died a millionaire, but he never would have been heard of even twenty years after his death. Do you know the names of any of Nineveh's millionaires? This man stepped out of that high position and took a low position, one upon which the world looked down upon and frowned, and his name has been associated with the walls of Jerusalem all these centuries.

Young man, if you want to be immortal, become identified with God's work, paying no attention to what people outside say. Nehemiah and his associates began at sunrise and worked until it grew so dark they could not see. A man who will take up God's work and work summer and winter throughout the year will have a harvest before the year is over, and the record of it will shine after he enters the next world.

The next thing we learn about Nehemiah is that he organized a great open-air meeting for the reading of the law of Moses in the hearing of the people. A pulpit of wood was built that was large enough to hold Ezra the scribe and thirteen others. The people wept when they heard the words of the law, but Nehemiah said, *Do not mourn nor weep. . . . Go, eat the fat, and drink sweet wine, and send portions unto those who have nothing prepared; for this day is holy unto our Lord, and not sad; for the joy of the LORD is your strength* (Nehemiah 8:9-10).

He did not forget the poor. Reading the Bible and remembering the poor – a combination of faith and works – will always bring joy.

Nehemiah then began to govern the city and correct the abuses he found existing. He gathered about fifty priests and scribes together and made them sign and seal a written covenant. Five things were in that covenant that I want to call attention to:

First, they were not to give their daughters to the heathen (Nehemiah 10:30). They had been violating the law of God and had been marrying their daughters to the ungodly. God had forbidden them to intermarry with the heathen nations in the land of Canaan, *for they will turn away thy son from following me that they may serve other gods; and the anger of the LORD will be kindled upon you and destroy thee suddenly* (Deuteronomy 7:4). I have known many people who have lost their power by being identified with the ungodly. If you want to have the blessing of God rest upon you, you must be very careful about your alliances. The Jews always got into trouble when they married with the nations around them. The houses of Ahab and Solomon lost their kingdoms by that sin. That was the cause of the overthrow of David's kingdom. Families who marry for wealth and marry the godly to the ungodly always bring distress into the family.

Next, Nehemiah made them sign a covenant that they would keep the Sabbath – that they would not buy on the Sabbath day. Think of this man who was brought up in the environment of a heathen court where they had no Sabbath, coming to Jerusalem and enforcing the law of Moses! It is recorded that they brought fish, and he would not let them into the city on the Sabbath, and the fish spoiled (Nehemiah 13:16-20). After they had tried that a few times, they gave up. If you will take your stand for God, even if you stand alone, it will not be long before you will get others to stand with you. God stood with Nehemiah, and He carried everything before him.

I don't believe we will have the right atmosphere in this country until we can get people who have enough backbone to stand up against what they believe is wrong. If it is a custom rooted and grounded for a hundred years, it doesn't matter; take your stand against it if you know it is wrong. If you have gatherings where it is fashionable to have wine and champagne, and you do not drink alcohol, if you are asked to go somewhere that will have alcohol, tell them you are not going.

A man asked me some years ago, "Mr. Moody, now that I am converted, must I give up the world?"

I said, "No, you don't have to give up the world. If you give a good sound testimony for the Son of God, the world will give you up pretty quick; they won't want you around."

There was going to be a great celebration at the opening of a saloon and billiard hall in Chicago – in the northern part of the city, where I lived. It was to be a gateway to death and hell – one of the worst places in Chicago. As a joke, they sent me an invitation to go to the opening. I took the invitation and went down and saw the two men who owned the saloon. I asked them, "Is this a genuine invitation?"

They said it was.

"Thank you," I said, "I will be around. If there is anything here I don't like, I may have something to say about it."

They said, "You are not going to preach, are you?"

"I may."

"We don't want you. We won't let you in."

"How are you going to keep me out?" I asked. "Here is the invitation."

"We will put a policeman at the door."

"What is the policeman going to do with that invitation?"

"We won't let you in."

"Well," I said, "I will be there."

I gave them a good scare, and then I said, "I will compromise the matter; if you two men will get down here and let me pray with you, I will let you off."

I got those two sellers of alcohol down on their knees, one on one side of me and the other on the other side, and I prayed to God to save their souls and smite their business. One of them had a Christian mother, and he seemed to have some conscience left. After I had prayed, I said, "How can you do this business? How can you throw this place open to ruin young men of Chicago?"

Within three months, the whole thing fell apart, and one of them was converted sometime after that. I have never been invited to a saloon since.

You won't have to give up the world, not by a long shot. If you go to reunions and there is drinking, simply get up and go away. You don't need to be a party to it. That is the kind of people we need. When you find anything that is ruining your fellow men, fight it to the bitter end.

Nehemiah said, "We will not have desecration of the Sabbath." Today, people freely break the Sabbath and wonder why they have no spiritual power.

The trouble today is that it doesn't mean anything to some people to be a Christian. What we must have is a higher type of Christianity in this country. We must have a Christianity that embraces the principle of self-denial. We must deny ourselves. If we want power, we must be separate.

The next thing the Israelites were to do (and bear

in mind, they had to sign this) – was to give their land rest. For four hundred and ninety years they had not let their land rest, so God took them away to Babylon for seventy years and let the land rest. A man who works seven days a week lives about five or ten years less. You cannot rob God. Why is it that so many railroad superintendents and physicians die early? It is because they work seven days a week. Nehemiah made them promise to keep the law of Moses. If the nations of the earth had kept that law, the truth would have gone to the four corners of the earth before now.

Nehemiah then made them sign a covenant that they would not charge usury. They were just grinding the poor down. I believe that the reason we are in such a wretched state in this country today is because of taking advantage of the poor and getting such a large amount of money from charging interest. People evade the law, pay the interest, and then they give a few hundred dollars to negotiate the loan. There is a great amount of usury, and see where we are today. See what a miserable state of things we are in, not only in this country, but all over the world.

The fifth thing he made them do was to bring their first fruits to the sons of Levi. They were to give God a tenth – the first and the best. As long as Israel did that, they prospered, and when they turned away from that law, they did not prosper. You can look through history and look around you and see the same thing today. As long as people keep God's law and respect God's testimony, they are going to prosper; but when they turn aside, like Samson, they lose their strength and have no power.

If you take these five things and carry them out, you will succeed in life and in following God. You may not necessarily be wealthy or even have an easy life, but you will be blessed and you will be in the will of God. Let us all do it personally. If it was good for those men, it is good for us. The moment we begin to rob God of time or talents, darkness and misery and wretchedness will come.

Chapter 5

Herod and John the Baptist

Dealing with Sin

If someone had told me a few years ago that he thought Herod was once near the kingdom of God, I would have been inclined to doubt it. I would have said, "I do not believe that the bloodthirsty wretch who took the life of John the Baptist ever had a serious thought in his life about his soul's welfare." I held that opinion because there is one scene recorded in Herod's life that I had overlooked. But some years ago, when I was making a careful study of the Gospel of Mark, I found this verse: *Herod feared John, knowing that he was a just man and holy man, and respected him; and when he heard him, he did many things and heard him gladly* (Mark 6:20).

This caused me to change my views about Herod. I saw that he was not only brought within the sound of John's voice, but under the power of the Spirit of God, his heart was touched and his conscience awakened. We are not told under what circumstances he heard

John, but the narrative plainly states that he was brought under the influence of the Baptist's wonderful ministry.

Let me first say a word or two about the preacher, John. I contend that John the Baptist must have been one of the most impressive preachers this world has ever had. Almost any man can get a hearing today in a town or a city where the people live close together, especially if he speaks in a fine building with a splendid choir and meetings that have been advertised and worked up for weeks or months beforehand. In such circumstances, any man who has a gift for speaking will get a good audience. But it was very different with John. He drew the people out of the towns and cities and into the wilderness. There were no ministers to back him, no businessmen interested in Christ's cause to work with him, and no newspaper reporters to write down his sermons and send them out. He was an unknown man without any title to his name. He was not the Right Reverend John the Baptist, D.D., or anything like that, but plain John the Baptist. When the people inquired of him whether he was Elijah or Jeremiah come back to life, he said he was not.

"Who are you then?"

"I am *the voice of one crying in the wilderness*" (Mark 1:3).

He was nothing but a voice – to be heard and not seen. He was Mr. Nobody. He regarded himself as a messenger who had received his commission from the eternal world.

We are not told how he began his ministry or how he gathered the crowds together. I can imagine that one day this strange man made his appearance in the valley of the Jordan, where he found a few shepherds tending their flocks. They brought their scattered sheep together, and the man preached to these shepherds. He told them that the kingdom of heaven was about to be set up on the earth, and he urged them to set their houses in order – to repent and turn from their sins. After he delivered his message, he might have told them that he would come back the next day and speak again.

When he had disappeared into the desert, I can suppose one of the shepherds saying to another, "Wasn't he a strange man? Did you ever hear anyone speak like that? He did not talk as the rabbis or the Pharisees or the Sadducees do. I really think he must be one of the old prophets. Did you notice that his coat was made of camel's hair and that he had a leather girdle around his loins? Don't the Scriptures say that Elijah was clothed like that?"

Another shepherd might have said, "Do you remember how Malachi said that before the great and dreadful day of the Lord, Elijah would come? I really believe this man is the old prophet of Carmel" (Malachi 4:5).

What could stir the heart of the Jewish people more than the name of Elijah? Word of John's appearance spread up and down the Jordan Valley, and when he returned the next day, there was great excitement and expectation as the people listened to the strange preacher. Perhaps until Christ came, John only preached from that one text: *Repent ye, for the kingdom of heaven is at hand* (Matthew 3:2). Day after day you could hear his voice ringing through the valley: "Repent! repent!

repent! The King is at the door. I do not know the day or the hour, but He will be here very soon."

Soon some of the people who flocked to hear him wanted to be baptized, and he took them to the Jordan and baptized them. The news spread to the surrounding villages and towns, and before long, it reached Jerusalem. Then the people of the city flocked to the desert to hear this prince among preachers. His fame reached Galilee, and the people in the mountains flocked down to hear him. Men left their fishing boats on the lake so they could listen to this wonderful preacher. When he was in the peak of his popularity, he may have had as many as twenty or thirty thousand people flock to his ministry day after day.

No doubt there were some old grumblers who said it was all sensation. "Catch me there? No, sir; I never did like sensational preaching." Just like today when any special effort is made to reach the people, some will say, "Much harm will be done."

I wish all these grumblers had died out with that generation in Judea, but we still have plenty of their descendants around. I venture to say you have met them. Why, my dear friends, there is more excitement in your whisky shops and beer saloons in one night than in all the churches put together in twelve months. What a stir there must have been in Israel under the preaching of John the Baptist and then of Christ! The whole country reeled and rocked with intense excitement. Don't be afraid of a little excitement in religious matters; it won't hurt.

One might have heard those old Pharisees and

scribes grumbling about John being such a sensational preacher, saying, "It won't last." And when Herod had John the Baptist beheaded, they would say, "Didn't I tell you so?"

We must not be in a hurry to pass judgment. John the Baptist lives today more than he ever did; his voice still rings throughout the world. He only preached a few months, but for more than nineteen hundred years his sermons have been repeated and multiplied, and the power of his words will never die as long as the world lasts.

I can imagine that when John was at the height of his popularity, as Herod sat in his palace in Jerusalem looking toward the Jordan Valley, he could see great crowds of people passing day after day. He began to ask what it meant, and the news came to him about this strange and powerful preacher. Perhaps someone reported that John was preaching treason – telling of a king who was at hand, getting ready to set up his kingdom.

"A king at hand! If Caesar were coming, I should have heard about it. There is no king but Caesar. I must look into the matter. I will go down to the Jordan and hear this man for myself."

So one day, as John stood preaching, with the eyes of the whole audience upon him, the people being swayed by his eloquence like treetops when the wind passes over them, all at once he lost their attention. All eyes were suddenly turned in the direction of the city. Someone might have cried, "Look, look! Herod is coming!"

Soon the whole congregation knew it, and there was great excitement.

"I believe he will stop this preaching," said another.

If they had been like some of the compromising, weak-kneed Christians we sometimes meet, they would have said to John, "Don't talk about a coming King; Herod won't stand for it. Talk about repentance, but any talk about a coming King will be high treason in the ears of Herod."

I think if anyone had dared to give John such counsel, John would have replied, "I have received my message from heaven; what do I care for Herod or anyone else?"

As he stood thundering away and calling on the people to repent, I can imagine Herod, with his guard of soldiers around him, listening attentively to find anything in the preacher's words that he could lay hold of. At last John said, "The King is now at the door. He will set up His kingdom and will separate the wheat from the chaff."

I can imagine Herod then saying to himself, "I will have that man's head off within twenty-four hours. I would arrest him here and now if I dared. I will catch him tomorrow before the crowd gathers."

As Herod listened, some of the people might have begun to press close to the preacher and question him. Some soldiers among them asked John, *What shall we do?*

John answered, *Oppress no one, neither accuse anyone falsely; and be content with your wages* (Luke 3:14).

"That is pretty good advice," Herod may have thought. "I have had a good deal of trouble with these men, but if they follow the preacher's advice, it will make them better soldiers."

Then he heard the publicans ask John, as they came to be baptized, *What shall we do?* (Luke 3:12).

John told them, *Exact no more than that which is appointed you* (Luke 3:13).

"Well," Herod may have said, "that is excellent advice. These publicans are always overtaxing the people. If they would do as the preacher tells them, the people would be more content."

Then the preacher addressed the Pharisees and the Sadducees in the crowd, crying out: *O generation of vipers, who taught you to flee from the wrath to come? Bring forth therefore fruits worthy of repentance* (Matthew 3:7-8).

Herod may have said to himself, "I like that. I am glad he is giving it pretty strong to these men. I don't think I will have him arrested just yet."

So he went back to his palace. I can imagine he was not able to sleep much that night; he kept thinking of what he had heard. When the Holy Spirit is dealing with a man's conscience, that person often cannot sleep. Herod probably could not get this wilderness preacher and his message out of his mind. The truth had reached his soul; it echoed and re-echoed within him: *Repent ye, for the kingdom of heaven is at hand.* Maybe he said, "I went out today to hear on behalf of the Roman government; I think I will go tomorrow and hear for myself."

He might have gone back again and again. My text says that he *heard him gladly*, that he observed him and feared him, *knowing that he was a just and holy man.* He must have known down in his heart that John was a heaven-sent messenger.

If you had gone into the palace in those days, you might have heard Herod talking of nobody but John the Baptist. He would say to his associates, "Have you been out to the desert to hear this strange preacher?"

"No; have you?"

"Yes."

"What? You, the Roman governor, going to hear this unordained preacher?"

"Yes, I have been there quite often. I would rather hear him than any man I ever knew. He doesn't talk like the regular preachers. I never heard anyone who had such influence over me."

You would have thought that Herod was a very hopeful subject. *He did many things.* Perhaps Herod stopped swearing. He may have stopped gambling and getting drunk. A wonderful change seemed to have passed over him. Perhaps he ceased from taking bribes for a while; we catch him at it afterwards, but maybe he temporarily refrained from it. He became quite virtuous in certain areas. It really looked as if he were near the kingdom of heaven.

I can imagine that one day, as John stood preaching, the truth was reaching the hearts and consciences of the people, and the powers of another world was falling upon them. One of John's disciples stood near Herod's chariot and saw the tears in the eyes of the Roman governor. At the close of the service, that disciple went to John and said, "I stood close to Herod today, and no one seemed more impressed. I could see the tears coming, and he had to brush them away to keep them from falling."

Have you ever seen a man in a religious meeting try to keep the tears back? You notice that his forehead seemed to itch, and he puts his hand up. You might know what it means; he wants to conceal the fact that the tears are there. He thinks it is a weakness, but it is not. Some people foolishly think it is not a weakness to get drunk and abuse their families, but that it is weakness to shed tears.

So this disciple of John may have noticed that Herod put his hand to his brow a number of times, not wanting his soldiers or those standing near to observe that he was weeping. The disciple said to John, "It looks as if he is coming near the kingdom. I believe you will have him as an inquirer very soon."

When a man enjoys hearing such a preacher, it certainly seems to be a hopeful sign. Herod might have been present that day Christ was baptized. Was there ever a man lifted so near to heaven as Herod must have been if he were present on that occasion? I can see John surrounded by a great throng of people who are hanging on his words. The eyes of the preacher, that never flinched before, suddenly began to look strange. He turned pale and seemed to draw back as though something wonderful had happened, and right in the middle of a sentence he ceased to speak.

If I were suddenly to grow pale and stop speaking, you would ask, "Has death crept onto the platform? Is the tongue of the speaker paralyzed?" There must have been quite a commotion among the audience when John stopped. The eyes of the Baptist were fixed upon a Stranger who pushed His way through the crowd. That Stranger came up to the preacher and requested to be baptized. That was a common occurrence; it had happened day after day for weeks past. John listened to the Stranger's words, but instead of going at once to the Jordan to baptize Him, he said, *I have need to be baptized of thee* (Matthew 3:14).

What a thrill of excitement must have shot through the audience. I can hear someone whispering to another, "I believe that is the Messiah." Yes, it was the long-looked-for One, for whose appearing the nation had been waiting thousands of years. From the time God had made the promise to Adam back in Eden, every true Israelite had been looking for the Messiah, and there He was in their midst!

He insisted that John should baptize Him, and the forerunner recognized His authority as Master, took Him to the Jordan River, and baptized Him. As Jesus came up from the water, the heavens opened, and the Spirit of God in the form of a dove descended and rested on Him (Matthew 3:16). When Noah sent forth the dove from the ark, it could find no resting place, but now the Son of God had come to do the will of God, and the dove found its resting place upon Him. The Holy Spirit had found a home. God broke the silence of four thousand years. There came a voice from heaven, and Herod may have heard it if he was there that day: *This is my beloved Son, in whom I am well pleased* (Matthew 3:17).

Even if Herod had not witnessed this scene and heard the voice, he must have heard about it, for the thing was not done in a corner. There were thousands to witness it, and the news must have been taken to every corner of the land.

Yet Herod, living in such times and hearing such a preacher, missed the kingdom of heaven in the end. He did many things because he feared John. Had he feared God, he would have done everything. *He did many things*, but there was one thing he would not do – he would not give up one treasured sin. The longer I preach, the more I am convinced that this is what keeps people out of the kingdom of God. John knew about Herod's private life and warned him in plain words.

If those compromising Christians of whom I have spoken had been near John, one of them would have said, "Look here, John; we hear that Herod is very anxious about his soul and is asking what he must do to be saved. Let me give you some advice. Don't mention Herod's secret sin. He is living with his brother's wife, but don't say anything about it, for he won't put up with that. He has the whole Roman government behind him, and if you allude to that matter, it will be more than your life is worth. You have a good chance with Herod now; he is afraid of you. Only be careful and don't go too far, or he will have your head cut off."

Some people are willing for you to preach about the sins of others, as long as you don't mention their own sins. My wife was once teaching my little boy a Sunday school lesson; she told him to notice how sin grows until it becomes a habit. The little fellow thought it was coming too close to him, so he turned red and finally said, "Momma, I think you are getting a good way from the subject."

John was a preacher of this uncompromising kind, for he drove the message right home. I do not know when or how the two were brought together at that time, but John kept nothing back. He boldly told Herod, *It is not lawful for thee to have thy brother's wife* (Mark 6:18).

The man was breaking the law of God and living in the cursed sin of adultery. Thank God, John did not spare him! It cost the preacher his head, but the Lord had his heart, and he did not care what became of his head. We read that Herod feared John, but John did not fear Herod.

I do not know of a quicker way to hell than by the way of adultery. Let no one think that he is going into the kingdom of God who does not repent of this sin in sackcloth and ashes. My friend, do you think God will not bring you into judgment? Doesn't the Bible say that no adulterer shall inherit the kingdom of God? *Know ye not that the unjust shall not inherit the kingdom of God? Do not err: neither fornicators nor idolaters nor adulterers nor effeminate nor homosexuals nor thieves nor covetous nor drunkards nor revilers nor extortioners shall inherit the kingdom of God* (1 Corinthians 6:9-10).

Do you think John the Baptist would have been a true friend of Herod if he had spared him and covered up his sin? Was it not a true sign that John loved him when he warned him and told him he must quit his sin? Herod had done many things before and heard John gladly, but he did not like him when John mentioned his sin. It is one thing to hear a man preach down other people's sins. People will say, "That was a great sermon," and they will want all their friends to go hear the preacher. But let that preacher deal with their own individual sin as John did, let him declare (as Nathan did to David), *Thou art the man* (2 Samuel 12:7), and they will say, "I don't like that." The preacher has touched a sore spot.

When a man has broken his arm, the surgeon must determine the exact spot of the fracture. He feels along and presses gently with his fingers.

"Is it there?"

"No."

"Is it there?"

"No."

Then the surgeon touches another spot. "Ouch!" says the man.

The doctor has found the broken part, and it hurts. John placed his finger on the fractured spot, and Herod winced under the pain. John put his hand right on it and said to Herod, *It is not lawful for thee to have thy brother Philip's wife.* Herod did not want to give up his sin.

Many people would be willing to enter into the kingdom of God if they could do it without giving up sin. People sometimes wonder why Jesus Christ, who lived six hundred years before Mohammed, has fewer disciples than Mohammed today. The explanation is not difficult. A man may become a disciple of Mohammed and continue to live in the foulest, darkest, deepest sin; but no one can be a disciple of Christ without giving up sin. If you are trying to make yourself believe that you can get into the kingdom of God without renouncing your sin, may God tear the mask from you! Can Satan persuade you that Herod will be found in the kingdom of God along with John the Baptist, with the sins of adultery and murder on his soul?

Now, let me say this. If your minister comes to you, tells you plainly of your sin, and warns you faithfully, thank God for him. He is your best friend; he is a heaven-sent man. But if a minister speaks smooth, oily words to you, tells you it is all right when you know, and he knows, that it is all wrong that we are living in sin, you may be sure that he is a devil-sent man.

I want to say I have contempt for a preacher who will tone down his message to suit someone in his audience – some senator or other important person. If the devil can get possession of such a minister and speak through him, that preacher will do the devil's work better than the devil himself.

You might be horrified if you knew Satan was deceiving you, but if a professed minister of Jesus Christ preaches this doctrine and says that God will make it all right in the end even though you go on living in sin, it is just the same. Don't be deluded into believing such doctrine – it is as false as any lie that ever came from the pit of hell. All the pastors and ministers of all the churches cannot save one soul that will not part with sin.

There is an old saying that every man has his price. Esau sold his birthright for a mess of pottage; pretty cheap, was it not? (Genesis 25:30-34). Ahab sold out for a garden of herbs (1 Kings 21:1-16). Judas sold out for thirty pieces of silver – less than seventeen dollars of our money (Matthew 26:14-15). Pretty cheap, was it not? Herod sold out for adultery.

What is the price that we might put on our soul? You say you do not know. I will tell you. It is the sin that keeps you from God. It might be alcohol; many people will give up the hope of heaven and sell their souls for alcohol. It may be immorality. Some say "Give me the harlot, and I will relinquish heaven with all its glories. I would rather be damned with my sin than saved without it."

What are you selling out for, my friend? You know what it is.

Wouldn't it have been a thousand times better for Herod today if he had taken the advice of John the Baptist instead of listening to that vile, adulterous woman? Herodias was pulling one way, John the other, and Herod was in the middle. It's the same old battle between right and wrong; heaven pulls one way, hell the other. Are you going to make the same mistake yourself?

We have ten thousand times more light than Herod had. He lived on the other side of the cross. The glorious gospel had not shone out as it has done since then. Think of the sermons you have heard and the entreaties addressed to you to become a Christian. Some of you have had godly mothers who have prayed for you. Many of you have godly wives who have pleaded with you and with God on your behalf. You have been surrounded with holy influences year after year; how often you have been near the kingdom of God! Yet here you are today, further off than ever!

It may be true of you, as it was of Herod, that you hear your preacher gladly. You attend church, contribute generously, and do many things. Remember that none of these activities will cleanse your soul from sin. They will not be accepted in place of what God demands – repentance and the forsaking of every sin.

A child was once playing with a vase, and he put his hand in but could not pull it out again. His father tried to help him, but in vain. At last he said, "Now, try once more. Open your fingers out straight and let me pull your arm."

"Oh, no, Papa," said the son. "I'd drop the penny if I opened my fingers like that."

Of course he couldn't get his hand out when his fist was closed, but he didn't want to give up the penny. It is the same with the sinner. He won't give up his sins to be free.

Your path and mine will perhaps never cross again, but if I have any influence with you, I urge you and plead with you to leave your sin now, whatever it might cost you. Herod might have been associated with Joseph of Arimathea and with the twelve apostles of the Lamb if he had taken the advice of John. There might have been a fragrance around his name all these centuries.

But alas! When we speak of Herod, we see a sneer on the faces of those who hear us. If one had asked Herod in those days, "Do you know that you are going to silence that great preacher and have him beheaded?" he would have replied, "Is your servant a dog that he should do such a thing? I never would take the life of such a man" (see 2 Kings 8:13). He would probably have thought he could never do it, yet only a little later he had the servant of God beheaded.

Do you know that the gospel of Jesus Christ proves to be either the savor of life unto life or of death unto death (2 Corinthians 2:16)? Sometimes we hear people say, "We will go and hear this man preach. If it does us no good, it will do us no harm." Don't you believe it, my friend. Every time you hear the gospel and reject it, the hardening process goes on. The same sun that melts the ice hardens the clay. The sermon that would have moved you a few years ago would make no impression now. Don't you remember a night when you heard a sermon that shook the foundations of your skepticism and unbelief? But now you are indifferent.

I believe Herod was seven times more a child of hell after his conviction had passed away than he was before. No true minister of the gospel will say that the hardest people to reach are those who have not been under conviction, but those whose conviction has worn away. It is much easier to commit a sin the second time than it was to commit it the first time, but it is much harder to repent the second time than the first.

If you are near the kingdom of God now, take the advice of a friend and step on into it. Don't be satisfied with just getting near. Jesus said to the young ruler, *Thou art not far from the kingdom of God*, but he failed to get there (Mark 12:34). Don't run any risks. If you put off a decision, death may overtake you before you have time to carry out your best intentions.

It is sad to think that people heard Jesus and Paul and were moved under their preaching, but were not saved. Judas must have come near the kingdom many times, but he never entered in. I saw it in the army – men who had almost decided to become Christians, cut down in battle without having taken the step that would have made them sure of eternal life. I confess there is something very sad about it.

A doctor was sent for from one of the tenement houses in New York City. He came and found a young man very sick. When the doctor approached the bedside, the young man said, "Doctor, I don't want you to deceive me. I want to know the worst. Is this illness to prove serious?"

After the doctor had examined the patient, he said: "I am sorry to tell you, but you cannot live out the night."

The young man looked up and said, "Well, then, I have missed it at last."

"Missed what?"

"I have missed eternal life. I always intended to become a Christian someday, but I thought I had plenty of time, and I put it off."

The doctor, who was himself a Christian, said, "It is not too late. Call on God for mercy."

"No," said the dying man. "I have always had great contempt for someone who repents when he is dying; he is a miserable coward. If I were not sick, I would not have a thought about my soul, and I am not going to insult God now."

The doctor spent the day with him, read to him out of the Bible, and tried to get him to lay hold of the promises. The young man said he would not call on God, and in that state of mind he passed away. Just as he was dying, the doctor saw his lips moving. He bent down, and all he could hear was the faint whisper, "I have missed it at last!"

Dear friend, make sure that you do not miss eternal life at last. Will you go with Herod or with John? Bow your head now and say, "Son of God, come into this heart of mine. I yield myself to Thee – fully, wholly, and unreservedly."

He will come to you and will not only save you, but He will keep you to the end.

Chapter 6

The Blind Man and Joseph of Arimathaea

Boldness

Two extraordinary men lived in the city of Jerusalem when Christ was on earth. One of them has come down through history nameless; we do not know who he was. The name of the other is given. One was not only a beggar, but he was blind from birth; the other was one of the rich men of Jerusalem. Yet in the Gospel of John, more space is given to this blind beggar than to any other character. Maybe the reason so much has been recorded of this man is that he took his stand for Jesus Christ.

In the eighth chapter of John, Jesus declared, *I AM the light of the world; he that follows me shall not walk in darkness but shall have the light of life* (John 8:12). Now consider the story of the blind man who was healed:

> *As long as I* [Jesus] *am in the world, I am the light of the world. When he had thus spoken, he spat on the ground and made clay of the spittle, and he anointed the eyes of the blind man with the clay and said unto him, Go, wash in the pool of Siloam (which is by interpretation, Sent). Then he went and washed and came back seeing.*
>
> *The neighbours, therefore, and those who before had seen him that he was blind said, Is not this he that sat and begged? Some said, This is he; others said, He is like him; but he said, I am he. Then they said unto him, How were thine eyes opened? He answered and said, A man that is called Jesus made clay and anointed my eyes and said unto me, Go to the pool of Siloam, and wash; and I went and washed, and I received sight.* (John 9:5-11)

Jesus had told them that He was the Light of the world, and if anyone would follow Him, he would not walk in darkness but would have the light of life. After making a statement like that, Christ often provided evidence of the truth of what He said by performing some miracle. If He had said He was the Light of the world, He would show them in what way He was the Light of the world.

If He had said He was the Life of the world, He would prove it by reviving and raising the dead, just as He did after telling them that He was the Resurrection and the Life and then went to the graveyard of Bethany and called Lazarus forth. When Lazarus heard the voice of his friend cry with a loud voice, *Lazarus, come forth,* he immediately came forth (John 11:43).

The Son of God does not ask people to believe Him without a reason for doing so. We need to keep this in mind. You might as well ask a man to see without light or eyes as to believe without testimony. Jesus gave them good reason for believing in Him, and He proved His Messiahship and authority. He not only told them that He had the power, but He showed them that He had it.

These two men, the blind man and Joseph of Arimathaea, were both at Jerusalem. One held as high a position and the other as low a position as any in the city. One was at the top of the social ladder and the other at the bottom, yet they both made a good confession. One was as acceptable to Jesus as the other.

The Blind Man

The man mentioned in this chapter was born blind, and we find the Lord's disciples asking Him, *Rabbi, who sinned, this man or his parents, that he was born blind? Jesus answered, Neither has this man sinned nor his parents; but that the works of God should be made manifest in him. When he had thus spoken, he spat on the ground and made clay of the spittle, and he anointed the eyes of the blind man with the clay and said unto him, Go, wash in the pool of Siloam* (John 9:2-3, 6-7).

The blind man went his way and washed, and his eyesight was restored. Observe what that man did. He did just what Christ told him to do. The Savior's command to him was to go to the pool of Siloam and wash; and *he went and washed and came back seeing* (John 9:7). He was blessed in the very act of obedience.

God does not generally repeat Himself. Of all the blind men who were healed while Christ was on earth, no two were healed in exactly the same way. Jesus met blind Bartimaeus near the gates of Jericho and called him and said, *What wilt thou that I should do unto thee? And the blind man said unto him, Master, that I might receive my sight* (Mark 10:51).

See what He did. He did not send Bartimaeus off to Jerusalem twenty miles away to the pool of Siloam to wash. He did not spit on the ground and make clay to anoint his eyes, but with a word He worked the cure, saying, *Go; thy faith has saved thee* (Mark 10:52).

Suppose Bartimaeus had gone from Jericho and had met the other blind beggar at the gate of the city of Jerusalem and asked him how he regained his sight. Suppose they began to compare notes – one telling his experience, and the other telling his. Imagine the first saying, "I do not believe that you have your sight, because you did not get it in the same way that I got mine."

Would the different ways the Lord Jesus healed them make their cases less true? Yet some people talk that way now. Because God does not deal with some people exactly as He does with others, people think that God is not dealing with them at all. God seldom repeats Himself. No two people were ever converted exactly alike, as far as my experience goes. Each one must have an experience of his own. Let the Lord give sight in His own way.

Thousands of people fail to meet Christ because they

are looking for the same experience of some dear friend or relative. They should not judge their conversion by the experiences of others. They have heard someone tell how he was converted twenty years ago, and they expect to be converted in the same way. People should never count on having an experience precisely the same as someone else whom they have heard about or read about. They must go to the Lord Himself and do what He tells them to do.

If He says, *Go, wash in the pool of Siloam,* then they must go. If He says, "Come" and promises to give sight, then they must come and let Him do His own work in His own way, just as this blind man did. Anointing a man's eyes with clay was a strange way to give him sight, but it was the Lord's way, and the man's sight was given to him.

We might think filling a man's eyes with clay was enough to make a man blind. True, he was now doubly blind, for if he had been able to see before, the clay would have deprived him of his sight. But the Lord wanted to show the people that they were not only spiritually blind by nature, but they had also allowed themselves to be blinded by the clay of this world, which had been spread over their eyes. God's ways are not our ways. If He is going to work, we must let Him act as He pleases.

Shall we dictate to the Almighty? *Shall the clay say to him that fashions it, What doth thou make; thy work has no form?* (Isaiah 45:9). *O man, who art thou to reply against God?* (Romans 9:20). Let God work in His own way, and when the Holy Spirit comes, let Him mark out a way for Himself. We must be willing to submit and do what the Lord tells us to do, without any questioning whatever.

Then he went and washed and came back seeing. The neighbours, therefore, and those who before had seen him that he was blind said, Is not this he that sat and begged? Some said, This is he; others said, He is like him (John 9:7-9). Now, if he had been like many people today, I am afraid he would have remained silent. He might have said, "Well, now I have my sight, but I will just keep quiet about it. It is not necessary for me to confess it. Why should I say anything? There is much opposition to this man Jesus Christ. Many bitter things are said in Jerusalem against Him. He has many enemies. I think there will be trouble if I talk about Him, so I will say nothing." *Some said, This is he; others said, He is like him; but he said, I am he.* The blind man not only got his eyes opened, but thank God, he got his mouth opened, too!

Surely, the next thing after we get our eyes opened is for us to open our lips and begin to testify for Him. The people asked the healed man, *How were thine eyes opened? He answered and said, A man that is called Jesus made clay and anointed my eyes and said unto me, Go to the pool of Siloam, and wash; and I went and washed, and I received sight* (John 9:10-11).

He told a straightforward story about what the Lord had done for him. That is all. That is what a witness ought to do – tell what he knows, not what he does not know. He did not try to make a long speech. It is not the most flippant and fluent witness who has the most influence with a jury.

This man's testimony is what I call experience. One of the greatest hindrances to the progress of the gospel today is that the narration of the experience of the Church is not encouraged. Many men and women come into the fold of Christ Jesus, but we never hear anything of their experiences or of the Lord's dealings with them. If we could, it would be a great help to others. It would stimulate faith and encourage the feebler of the flock.

The apostle Paul's experience has been recorded three times. I have no doubt that he told it everywhere he went: how God had met him, how God had opened his eyes and his heart, and how God had blessed him. Experience has its place, but the great mistake that is made now is in the other extreme. In some places and at some periods there has been too much significance put on it. Testimonies have become all experience, and the pendulum has swung too far the other way.

But appropriately, I think it is not only right, but exceedingly useful to describe our experience. The blind man bore testimony to what the Lord had done for him:

> *And it was the sabbath day when Jesus had made the clay and had opened his eyes. Then again the Pharisees also asked him how he had received his sight. He said unto them, He put clay upon my eyes, and I washed and do see. Therefore some of the Pharisees said, This man is not of God because he does not keep the sabbath day. Others said, How can a man that is a sinner do such signs?*

> *And there was a division among them. They said unto the blind man again, What sayest thou of him, that has opened thine eyes?* (John 9:14-17)

What an opportunity he had for evading the questions! He could have said, "Why, I have never seen Him. When He met me, I was blind; I could not see Him. When I came back, I could not find Him, and I have not formed any opinion yet." He might have put them off in that way, but he said, *He is a prophet* (John 9:17). He gave them his opinion. He was a man of backbone. He had moral courage. He stood right up among the enemies of Jesus Christ, the Pharisees, and told them what he thought of Him: *He is a prophet.*

If you can get young Christians to talk, not about themselves, but about Christ, their testimony will have power. Many converts talk altogether about their own experience. They say, "I," "I," "I," "I." But this blind man got away from the Master and said, *He is a prophet.* He believed, and he told them what he believed.

> *But the Jews did not believe concerning him that he had been blind and received his sight until they called the parents of him that had received his sight. And they asked them, saying, Is this your son, who ye say was born blind? How then does he now see?*
>
> *His parents answered them and said, We know that this is our son and that he was born blind; but by what means he now sees, we know not; or who has opened his eyes,*

> *we know not; he is of age, ask him; he shall speak for himself. These words spoke his parents because they feared the Jews, for the Jews had agreed already that if anyone did confess that he was Christ, he should be put out of the synagogue. Therefore his parents said, He is of age, ask him.* (John 9:18-23)

I have always had great disrespect for those parents. They had a noble son, and their lack of moral courage right then to confess what the Lord Jesus Christ had done for their son makes them unworthy of him. They said, "We do not know how he was healed," which looks as if they did not believe their own son. *He is of age, ask him,* they said.

It is sorrowfully true today that we have hundreds and thousands of people who are professing disciples of Jesus Christ, but when the time comes for them to take their stand and give a clear testimony for Him, they testify against Him. You can always tell those who are really converted to God. The new man always takes his stand for God, but the old man takes his stand against Him. These parents had an opportunity to confess the Lord Jesus Christ and to do great things for Him, but they neglected their golden opportunity.

If they had just stood up with their honorable son and said, "This is our son. We have tried all the physicians and used all the means in our power, but were unable to help him; but now, out of gratitude, we confess that he received his sight from the prophet of Galilee, Jesus of Nazareth," they might have led many to believe in Him. Instead of that, they said, *We know that this is our son and that he was born blind; but by what means he now sees, we know not.*

Do you know why they did not want to tell how he got his sight? Simply because it would cost them too much. They represent those Christians who do not want to serve Christ if it is going to cost them anything. They do not want to give up society, position, or worldly pleasures. They do not want to be separate from the world. This keeps hundreds and thousands from becoming true Christians.

To be put out of the synagogue in those days was a serious thing. It does not mean so much now. If someone is put out of one church now, another may receive him; but when a man was put out of the synagogue at that time, there was no other to take him in. It was like a state church; it was the only one they had. If he were cast out of that, he was cast out of society, position, and everything else; even his business suffered.

The Jews *called again the man that had been blind and said unto him, Give glory to God; we know that this man is a sinner* (John 9:24). It looks as if they were trying to prejudice him against Christ, but *he answered and said, Whether he is a sinner or not, I do not know; one thing I know, that having been blind, now I see* (John 9:25).

No infidels or philosophers there could persuade him differently. There were not enough people in Jerusalem to make him believe that his eyes were not opened. Did he not know that for more than twenty years he had been feeling his way around Jerusalem, that he had been led by children and friends, and that during all those years he had not seen the sun in its glory or any of the beauties of nature? Didn't he know that he had been feeling his way through life until that very day?

Do we not know that we have been born of God and that the eyes of our souls have been opened? Do we not know that old things have passed away, all things have become new, and eternal light has dawned upon our souls? Do we not know that the chains that once bound us have snapped apart, the darkness is gone, and the light has come? Don't we have liberty where we once had bondage? Don't we know it?

If so, then let us not hold our peace. Let us testify for the Son of God and say, as the blind man did in Jerusalem, "*One thing I know, that having been blind, now I see.* I have a new power. I have a new light. I have a new love. I have a new nature. I have something that reaches out toward God. By the eye of faith, I can see heaven beyond. I can see Christ standing at the right hand of God. By and by, when my journey is over, I am going to hear that voice saying, *Come up here* [Revelation 4:1, 11:12], and I shall sit down in the kingdom of God."

Then said they to him again, What did he do to thee? How did he open thine eyes? He answered them, I have told you already, and ye have heard; what more would ye hear? Do ye also desire to be his disciples? (John 9:26-27). This was a most extraordinary man. Here was a young convert in Jerusalem, not a day old, trying to make converts of these Pharisees – men who had been fighting Christ for nearly three years! He asked them if they also wanted to become His disciples. He was ready to tell his experience to all who were willing to listen. If he had covered it up at first and had not told his experience at once, he would not have had the privilege of testifying in that way, nor would he have been a winner of souls. This man was going to be a soul winner.

I venture to say he became one of the best workers in Jerusalem. I have no doubt he stood well to the front on the day of Pentecost, when Peter preached and when the wounded were around him. He went to work and told how the Lord had blessed him, and how He would bless them. He was a worker, not an idler, and he continued to speak.

It is a very sad thing that so many of God's children are mute, yet it is true. Parents would think it was a great calamity to have their children born mute. They would mourn over it and weep, and they might rightly be sad, but did you ever think of the many speechless children God has? The churches are full of them; they never speak for Christ. They can talk about politics, sports, and science; they can speak well enough and fast enough about the entertainment of the day, but they have no voice for the Son of God.

Dear friend, if He is your Savior, confess Him. Every follower of Jesus should bear testimony for Him. We have many opportunities in society and in business to speak a word for Jesus Christ. Many opportunities occur daily where every Christian might *be instant in season and out of season* in pleading for Jesus (2 Timothy 4:2). As we do this, we receive blessing for ourselves and become a means of blessing to others.

This man wanted to make converts of those Pharisees who had recently been ready with their hands full of stones – ready to put the Son of God to death – and even now had murder in their hearts. *Then they reviled him and said. Be thou his disciple, but we are disciples of Moses. We know that God spoke unto Moses; as for this fellow, we do not know where he is from* (John 9:28-29).

The once-blind man might have said, "There is a good deal of opposition, and I will say no more; I will keep quiet and walk off and leave them." Thank God, he stood right up with the courage of a Paul. He answered and said unto them, *Indeed this is a marvellous thing that ye do not know where he is from, and yet he has opened my eyes. Now we know that God does not hear sinners, but if anyone should fear God and do his will, him he will hear* (John 9:30-31).

Now I call that logic. If he had been through a theological seminary, he could not have given a better answer. It is sound doctrine and a good sermon for those who were opposed to the work of Christ. *If this man were not of God, he could do nothing* (John 9:33). This is very strong proof of the man's conviction as to who the Lord Jesus was. It is as though he said: "I am a man who was born blind, and He can give me sight. He a sinner?" Why, it is unreasonable. If Jesus Christ were only a man, how could He give that man sight? Let philosophers, skeptics, and infidels answer the question.

He did not have to wear glasses, either. He received good sight – not short sight or weak sight – but sight as good as any man in Jerusalem, and perhaps a little better. They could all look at him and see for themselves. His testimony was beyond dispute.

After his splendid confession of the divinity and

power of Christ, *they answered and said unto him, Thou wast altogether born in sins, and dost thou teach us? And they cast him out* (John 9:34). They could not meet his argument, so they cast him out. That is how it is now. If we give a clear testimony for Christ, the world will cast us out. It is a good thing to give our testimony so clearly for Christ that the world dislikes it. It is a good thing, too, when such a testimony for Christ causes the world to cast us out.

What happened when they cast him out? *Jesus heard* – that is the next thing. No sooner did they cast him out than Jesus heard of it. No one was ever cast out by the world for the sake of Jesus Christ without Him hearing of it; indeed, He will be the first one to hear of it. *Jesus heard that they had cast him out; and finding him, he said unto him, Dost thou believe in the Son of God? He answered and said, Who is he, Lord, that I might believe in him? And Jesus said unto him, Thou hast seen him, and it is he that talks with thee. And he said, Lord, I believe. And he worshiped him* (John 9:35-38).

That was a good place to leave him – at the feet of Jesus. We will meet him again in the kingdom of God. His testimony has been told through the ages for two thousand years. It has been talked about wherever the Word of God has been known. That man did a wonderful day's work for the Son of God. There will certainly be many in eternity who will thank God for the blind man's confession of Christ.

By showing his gratitude in publicly confessing Christ, he has left a record that has stirred the Church of

God ever since. He is one of the characters that always stirs people up and imparts new life and fire and new boldness and courage when one reads about him. This is what we need today as much as ever – to stand up for the Son of God. Let the Pharisees rage against us. Let the world go on mocking and sneering and scoffing. We will stand up courageously for the Son of God. If they cast us out, they will cast us right into Christ. He will take us to His own loving arms. It is a blessed thing to live so godly in Christ Jesus that the world will not want you – that they will cast you out.

Joseph of Arimathaea

I do not think Joseph of Arimathaea came out as a follower of Jesus as nobly as this blind beggar did, but he did come out, and we will thank God for that. We read in John that for fear of the Jews he was kept back from confessing openly: *After these things, Joseph of Arimathaea, being a disciple of Jesus but secretly for fear of the Jews, besought Pilate that he might take away the body of Jesus, and Pilate gave him leave. He came therefore and took the body of Jesus* (John 19:38).

Read the four accounts of Joseph of Arimathaea given in the four gospels:

Matthew 27:57-60

> *When the evening was come, there came a rich man of Arimathaea, named Joseph, who also had been a disciple of Jesus; he went to Pilate and asked for the body of Jesus. Then Pilate*

commanded the body to be delivered. And when Joseph had taken the body, he wrapped it in a clean linen cloth and laid it in his own new tomb, which he had hewn out in the rock, and he rolled a great stone to the door of the sepulchre and departed.

Mark 15:42-46

And now when the evening was come, because it was the preparation, that is, the day before the sabbath, Joseph of Arimathaea, a noble senator, who also waited for the kingdom of God, came and went in boldly unto Pilate and asked for the body of Jesus. And Pilate marvelled that he was already dead; and calling unto him the centurion, he asked him whether he was already dead. And when he knew it of the centurion, he gave the body to Joseph. And he bought fine linen and took him down and wrapped him in the linen and laid him in a sepulchre which was hewn out of a rock and rolled a stone unto the door of the sepulchre.

Luke 23:50-53

And, behold, there was a man named Joseph, a senator; and he was a good man and just (the same had not consented in the counsel nor in their deeds); he was of Arimathaea, a city of Judea, who also himself waited for the kingdom of God. This man went unto Pilate and asked for the body of Jesus. And he took it down and wrapped it in linen and laid it in a sepulchre that was hewn in stone, where no one had ever been placed.

John 19:38-42

After these things, Joseph of Arimathaea, being a disciple of Jesus but secretly for fear of the Jews, besought Pilate that he might take away the body of Jesus, and Pilate gave him leave. He came therefore and took the body of Jesus. Then Nicodemus came also, who at the first came to Jesus by night, and brought a mixture of myrrh and aloes, about one hundred pounds. And they took the body of Jesus and wound it in linen clothes with the spices, as is the manner of the Jews to bury. Now in the place where he was crucified there was a garden, and in the garden a new sepulchre, in which no one had yet been laid. Therefore they laid Jesus there because of the Jews' preparation day, for the sepulchre was near.

There is very little mentioned by all four of the Evangelists. If Matthew and Mark refer to an event, it is often omitted by Luke and John. If it occurs in Luke or John, it may not be found in Matthew and Mark. John's Gospel is made up of that which is absent from the others in most instances – as in the case of the blind man alluded to in John 9:1-12. However, all four record what Joseph of Arimathaea did for Christ. All of

Jesus' disciples had forsaken Him. One had sold Him and another had denied Him. He was left in gloom and darkness, when Joseph of Arimathaea came out and confessed Him.

It was the death of Jesus Christ that brought out Joseph of Arimathaea. Probably he was one of the people who stood at the cross when the centurion struck his breast and cried out, *Truly, this man was the Son of God* (Mark 15:39), and he was doubtless convinced at the same time. Joseph was a disciple before, because we read that on the night of the trial he did not give his consent to the death of Christ. Imagine the surprise in the council chamber that night when Joseph of Arimathaea, a rich man, stood up and said, "I will never give my consent to His death."

There were seventy councilmen, but we have good reason to believe that two of them, like Caleb and Joshua of old, had the courage to stand up for Jesus Christ. These two men were Joseph of Arimathaea and Nicodemus. Neither of them gave their consent to the death of Christ, but I am afraid that Joseph did not then profess to be a disciple, for we do not find a word said about his being one until after the crucifixion.

I am afraid there are many Josephs today, men of position who are secret disciples. Such people would probably say today, "I do not need to take my stand on Christ's side. What more do I need? I have everything." We read that Joseph was a rich and honorable councilman, a just and good man who held a high position in the government of the nation. He was a benevolent and devout man, too. What more could he need? God wants something more than Joseph's good life and high position. A man might be all that Joseph was and yet be without Christ.

A crisis came in his history, though. If Joseph was to take his stand, this was the time for him to do it. I consider this one of the grandest, noblest acts that any man ever did – to take his stand for Christ when there seemed nothing, humanly speaking, that Christ could give him. Joseph had no hope concerning the resurrection. It seems that none of our Lord's disciples understood that He was going to rise again. Even Peter, James, and John, as well as the rest, scarcely believed He had risen when He appeared to them. They had anticipated that He would set up His kingdom, but He had no scepter in His hand, and as far as they could determine, He had no kingdom in view. In fact, He was dead on the cross with nails through His hands and feet. There He hung until His Spirit took its flight; that which had made Him so grand, so glorious, and so noble had now left the body.

Joseph might have said, "It will be no use taking a stand for Him now. If I step forward and confess Him, I will probably lose my influence and my position in society and in the council. I had better remain where I am." There was no earthly reward for him. There was nothing, humanly speaking, that could have induced him to proclaim his faith in Jesus; yet we are told by Mark that he went boldly into Pilate's judgment hall and begged for the body of Jesus.

I consider this one of the grandest and noblest acts that anyone ever did. In that darkness and gloom,

Jesus' disciples had all forsaken Him. Judas had sold Him for thirty pieces of silver. The chief apostle, Peter, had denied Him with a curse and swore that he never knew Him. The chief priests had found Him guilty of blasphemy, and the council had condemned him to death. When there was a hiss going up to heaven over all Jerusalem, Joseph went right against the current, against the influence of all his friends, and begged for the body of Jesus.

Blessed act! Doubtless he upbraided himself for not having been bolder in his defense of Christ when He was tried and before He was condemned to be crucified. The Scripture says that Joseph of Arimathaea was an honorable man, an honorable councilor, and a rich man, yet we only have the record of that one thing – the one act of begging for the body of Jesus. I tell you, though, that what he did for the Son of God, out of pure love for Him, will live forever. That one act rises above everything else that Joseph of Arimathea ever did. He might have given large sums of money to different institutions. He might have been generous to the poor. He might have been kind to the needy in various ways; but that one act for Jesus Christ on that memorable, dark afternoon was one of the noblest acts that anyone ever did. He must have been a man of great influence, or Pilate would not have given him the body.

Now let's look at Nicodemus, another secret disciple. Nicodemus and Joseph both went to the cross. Joseph was there first, and while he was waiting for Nicodemus to come, he looked down the hill. I can imagine his delight as he saw his friend coming with a hundred pounds of ointment. Although Jesus Christ had led such a lowly life, He was to have a kingly anointing and burial. God had touched the hearts of these two noble men, and they drew out the nails and took the body down. They washed the blood away from the wounds that had been made on His back from the scourging, and on His head from the crown of thorns. Then they took the lifeless form, washed it clean, wrapped it in fine linen, and Joseph laid Him in his own sepulcher.

When all was dark and gloomy, when His cause seemed to be lost and the hope of the Church was buried in that new tomb, Joseph took his stand for the One *despised and rejected among men* (Isaiah 53:3). It was the greatest act of his life. If you want to stand with the Lord Jesus Christ in glory, if you want the power of God to be bestowed upon you for service, then you must not hesitate to take your stand boldly and strongly for the most despised of all men – the Man Christ Jesus.

His cause is unpopular. The ungodly sneer at His name. But if you want the blessings of heaven on your soul, and if you want to hear the *Well done, good and faithful slave . . . enter thou into the joy of thy lord* (Matthew 25:23), you must take your stand at once for Him, whatever your position may be or how much your friends may be against you. Decide for Jesus Christ, the crucified but risen Savior. Go outside the camp and bear His reproach. Take up your cross and follow Him, and someday you will lay it down and take the crown to wear forever.

I remember some meetings being held in a locality where the tide did not rise very quickly, and bitter and reproachful things were being said about our work. But one day, one of the most prominent men in the place rose and said, "I want it to be known that I am a disciple of Jesus Christ, and if there is any hatred to be cast on His cause, I am prepared to take my share of it."

Those words went through the meeting like an electric current, and a blessing came at once to his own soul and to the souls of others. Depend upon it; there is no crown without a cross.

We must take our proper position here, as Joseph did. It cost him something to take up his cross. I have no doubt they put him out of the council and out of the synagogue. He lost his standing, and perhaps his wealth. Like other faithful followers of Christ, he became a despised and unpopular man.

The blind man could not have done what Joseph did. Some people can do what others cannot. God will hold us responsible for our own influence. Let each of us do what we can. Even though the conduct of our Lord's professed followers was anything but helpful to those who, like Joseph, had only a little courage to take a stand on the Lord's side, he was not deterred from taking his stand.

Whatever it costs us, let us be true Christians and take a firm stand. It is like the dust in the balance in comparison to what God has in store for us. We can afford to suffer with Him for a little while if we are going to reign with Him forever. We can afford to take up the cross and follow Him and be despised and rejected by the world since we have such a bright prospect in view.

If the glories of heaven are real, it will be to His praise and to our advantage to share in His rejection now.

May the Lord keep us from hesitating, and may we not be found wanting when weighed in the balances (see Daniel 5:27). May God help every reader to do all that the poor blind beggar did and all that Joseph did.

Let us confess Him at all times and in all places. Let us show our friends that we are totally and completely on His side. Everyone has a circle that he can influence, and God will hold us responsible for the influence we possess. Joseph of Arimathea and the blind man had circles in which their influence was powerful. I can influence people that others cannot reach. They, in turn, can reach a group that I could not touch. It is only for a little while that we can confess Him and work for Him. It is only for a few months or years, and then the eternal ages will roll on, and great will be our reward in the crowning day that is coming. We will then hear the Master say to us: *Well done, good and faithful slave . . . enter thou into the joy of thy lord.*

God grant that it may be so!

Chapter 7

The Penitent Thief

It's Not Too Late

It should give us all a great deal of hope and comfort that Jesus saved such a man as the penitent thief just before He went back to heaven. Everyone who is not a Christian ought to be interested in this case in order to learn how he was converted. Anyone who does not believe in sudden conversions ought to look into it. If conversions are gradual, if it takes six months, six weeks, or six days to convert someone, then this thief had no chance. If someone who has lived a good, consistent life cannot be converted suddenly, how much less chance for the thief. In the twenty-third chapter of Luke, we see how the Lord dealt with him:

> *And one of the malefactors which were hanged railed on him, saying, If thou art the Christ, save thyself and us. But the other answering rebuked him, saying, Dost not thou fear*

> *God, seeing thou art in the same condemnation? And we indeed justly, for we receive the due reward of our deeds; but this man has done nothing amiss. And he said unto Jesus, Lord, remember me when thou comest into thy kingdom. And Jesus said unto him, Verily I say unto thee, Today shalt thou be with me in paradise.* (Luke 23:39-43)

He was a thief, and the worst kind of a thief, or they would not have punished him by crucifixion. Jesus not only saved him, but He took him with Him into paradise.

Christ hung on the cross between the two thieves. The scribes and Pharisees shook their heads and jeered at Him. His disciples had fled. Only His mother and one or two other women remained in sight to cheer Him with their presence among all the crowd of enemies. Hear those spiteful Pharisees mocking among themselves: *He saved others; let him save himself if he is the Christ, the chosen of God* (Luke 23:35). The account also says that the two thieves *reproached him with the same* (Matthew 27:44).

Reviling

The first thing we read of this man is that he was a reviler of Christ. You would think that he would be doing something else at such a time as that; but hanging there in the midst of torture, certain to be dead in a few hours, instead of confessing his sins and preparing to meet that God whose law he had broken all his life, he is mistreating God's only Son. Surely, he cannot sink any lower, until he sinks into hell!

Under Conviction

The next time we hear of this thief, he appears to be under conviction: *And one of the malefactors which were hanged railed on him, saying, If thou art the Christ, save thyself and us. But the other answering rebuked him, saying, Dost not thou fear God, seeing thou art in the same condemnation? And we indeed justly; for we receive the due reward of our deeds; but this man has done nothing amiss* (Luke 23:39-41).

What do you suppose made such a great change in this man in these few hours? Jesus had not preached a sermon and had given him no exhortation. The darkness had not yet come on. The earth had not opened her mouth. The business of death was going on undisturbed. The crowd was still there, mocking and hissing and shaking their heads. Yet this man, who in the morning was denouncing Christ, confessed his sins and rebuked the other thief. *We indeed justly.* No miracle had been performed before his eyes. No angel from heaven had come to place a glittering crown upon Jesus' head in place of the bloody crown of thorns.

What caused such a change in him? I will tell you what I think it was. I think it was the Savior's prayer: *Father, forgive them; for they know not what they do* (Luke 23:34). I can almost hear the thief talking to himself in this way:

"What a strange kind of man this must be. He claims to be king of the Jews, and the writing over His cross says the same. But what sort of a throne is this? He says He is the Son of God. Why doesn't God send down His angels and destroy all these people who are torturing His Son to death? If He has all power now, as He used to have when He worked those miracles they talk about, why doesn't He bring out His vengeance and sweep all these wretches into destruction? I would do it in a minute if I had the power. I wouldn't spare any of them. I would open the earth and swallow them up. But this man prays to God to forgive them. Strange, strange! He *must* be different from us. I am sorry I said one word against Him when they first hung us up here.

"What a difference there is between Him and me. Here we are, hanging on two crosses, side by side; but all the rest of our lives we have been far enough apart. I have been robbing and murdering, and He has been feeding the hungry, healing the sick, and raising the dead. Now these people are denouncing us both. I am beginning to believe He must be the Son of God, for surely no man could forgive his enemies like that."

Yes, that prayer of Christ's did what the scourge could not do. This man had gone through his trial, had been beaten, and had been nailed to the cross; but his heart had not been subdued. He had raised no cry to God, and he was not sorry for his sins; yet when he heard the Savior praying for His murderers – that broke his heart.

It flashed into this thief's soul that Jesus was the Son of God, and that moment he rebuked his companion, saying, *Dost thou not fear God?* The fear of God fell upon him. A man has little hope of being saved until the fear of God comes upon him. Solomon says, *The fear of the LORD is the beginning of wisdom* (Proverbs 9:10).

We read in Acts that great fear fell upon the people; that was the fear of the Lord. That fear was the first sign that conviction had entered the soul of the thief. *Dost thou not fear God?* That was the first sign we have of life springing up.

Confession

Next, he confessed his sins: *We indeed justly.* He took his place among sinners, not trying to justify himself. A person may be very sorry for his sins, but if he doesn't confess them, he has no promise of being forgiven. Cain felt badly enough over his sins, but he did not confess them (Genesis 4). Saul was greatly tormented in mind, but he went to the witch of Endor instead of to the Lord (1 Samuel 28). Judas felt so bad over the betrayal of his Master that he went out and hanged himself, but he did not confess to God (Matthew 27:3-5). True, he went and confessed to the priests, saying, *I have sinned in that I have betrayed the innocent blood*, but it was of no use to confess to them, for they could not forgive him.

How different is the case of this penitent thief! He confessed his sins, and Christ had mercy on him immediately. The great trouble is that people are always trying to make out that they are not sinners and have nothing to confess. Therefore, there is no chance of reaching them with the gospel. There is no hope for a man who folds his arms and says, "I don't think God will punish sin; I am going to take the risk." There is no hope for a man until he sees that he is under just condemnation for his sins and shortcomings. God never forgives a sinner until he confesses.

Justifying Christ

Next, the thief justifies Christ: *This man has done nothing amiss.* When people are talking against Christ, they are far from becoming Christians. Now this man says, *He has done nothing amiss.* The world was mocking him, but in the midst of it all you could hear that thief crying out, "This Man has done nothing wrong."

Faith

The next step is faith. Talk about faith! I think this is about the most extraordinary case of faith in the Bible. Abraham was the father of the faithful, but God had him in training for twenty-five years. Moses was a man of faith, but he saw the burning bush and had other evidences of God. Elijah had faith, but he had good reason for it. God took care of him and fed him in time of famine.

Here was a man who perhaps had never seen a miracle. He had spent his life among criminals. His friends were thieves and outlaws, and he was now in his dying agonies in the presence of a crowd that was rejecting and reviling the Son of God. Jesus' disciples, who had heard His wonderful words and witnessed His mighty works, had forsaken Him. Perhaps the thief knew this. Peter had denied Him with oaths and cursing, and the thief might have known about this, too. Judas had betrayed Him.

He saw no glittering crown upon His brow, but

only the crown of thorns. He could see no sign of His kingdom. Where were His subjects? Yet, nailed to the cross, racked with pain in every nerve, overwhelmed with horror, his wicked soul in a tempest of passion, this thief managed to lay hold of Christ and trust Him for a swift salvation. The faith of this thief flashed out amid the darkness of Calvary. It is one of the most astounding instances of faith in the Bible.

When I was a boy, I was a poor speller. One day the boy at the head of the class was asked to spell a word, but he couldn't spell it, and none of our classmates could spell it. I spelled it, by good luck, and I went from the bottom of the class to the head. In the same way, the thief on the cross passed by Abraham, Moses, and Elijah and went to the head of the class. *He said unto Jesus, Lord, remember me when thou comest into thy kingdom* (Luke 23:42).

Thank God for such a faith! How refreshing it must have been to Christ to have one person confess Him as Lord and believe in His kingdom at that dark hour. How this thief's heart went out to the Son of God! How glad he would have been to fall on his knees at the foot of the cross and pour out his prayer! But this he couldn't do. His hands and feet were nailed fast to the wood, but they had not nailed his eyes and his tongue and his heart. He could at least turn his head and look upon the Son of God, and his breaking heart could go out in love to the One who was dying for him and dying for you and me. He could say, *Lord, remember me when thou comest into thy kingdom.*

What a confession of Christ that was! He called

Him *Lord.* What a strange Lord! Nails through His hands and feet, fastened to the cross. What a strange throne! Blood was trickling down His face from the scars made by the crown of thorns, but He was all the more Lord because of this.

Sinner – call Him *Lord* now! Take your place as a poor condemned rebel, and cry out, *Lord, remember me!* That isn't a very long prayer, but it will prevail. We don't have to add *when thou comest into thy kingdom*, because Christ is now at His Father's right hand. Three words – a chain of three golden links that will bind the sinner to his Lord.

Some people think they must have a written prayer or a prayer book if they are going to address the throne of grace properly. But what could that poor fellow have done with a prayer book up there, hanging on the cross with both hands nailed fast? Suppose it had been necessary for some priest or minister to pray for him; what could he do? Nobody was there to pray for him, and yet he was going to die in a few hours. Man could not help him, but God had provided help from One who is mighty, and that One was close at hand. The thief prayed from his heart. His prayer was short, but it brought the blessing. It was right to the point: *Lord, remember me when thou comest into thy kingdom.* He asked the Lord to give him, right then and there, what he wanted.

The Answered Prayer

Now consider the answer to his prayer. He got more than he asked for, just as everyone does who asks in faith. He only asked Christ to *remember* him, but Christ answered, *Today shalt thou be with me in paradise* (Luke 23:43).

Immediate blessing – promise of fellowship – eternal rest; this is the way Christ answered his prayer.

Darkness

Then darkness fell upon the earth. The sun hid itself. Worst of all, the Father hid His face from His Son. What else is the meaning of that bitter cry: *My God! my God! Why hast Thou forsaken me?* (Matthew 27:46).

Oh, but it had been written, *Cursed is every one that hangs on a tree* (Galatians 3:13). Jesus was made a curse for us. God cannot look upon sin, so even when His own Son bore our sins in His body, God could not look upon Him.

I think this is what weighed heaviest upon the Savior's heart in the garden when He prayed, *If it be possible, let this cup pass from me* (Matthew 26:39).

He could bear the unfaithfulness of His friends, the enmity of His enemies, the pain of His crucifixion, and the shadow of death. He could bear all these, but when it came to His Father hiding His face, that seemed too much for even the Son of God to bear. But even this He endured for our sins. Now the face of God is turned back to us, whose sins had turned it away, and looking upon Jesus, the sinless One, He saw us in Him.

In the midst of all His agony, how sweet it must have been to Christ to hear that poor thief confessing Him. He takes pleasure in people who confess Him. Do you remember Jesus asking His disciples, *Who do men say that I the Son of man am?* When they answered, *Some say that thou art John the Baptist; some, Elijah; and others Jeremiah or one of the prophets,* He asked, *But who say ye that I am?* When Peter said, *Thou art the Christ, the Son of the living God,* Jesus blessed him for that confession (Matthew 16:13-19).

This thief confessed Jesus as Messiah. He confessed Him in the darkness. Perhaps it was so dark he couldn't see Him any longer, but he felt Jesus there beside him. Christ wants us to confess Him in the dark as well as in the light – when things are difficult as well as when things are easy. He was not ashamed of us, but He bore our sins and carried our sorrows, even unto death.

When a prominent man dies, we are anxious to know about his last words and acts. The last act of the Son of God was to save a sinner. That was a part of the glory of His death. He began His ministry by saving sinners, and He ended it by saving this poor thief. *Shall the prey be taken from the mighty, or the lawful captive delivered? But thus saith the LORD, Even the captives of the mighty shall be taken away, and the prey of the terrible shall be delivered* (Isaiah 49:24-25). Jesus took this captive from the jaws of death. He was on the borders of hell, and Christ snatched him away.

No doubt, Satan was saying to himself, "I will have the soul of that thief pretty soon. He belongs to me. He has been mine all these years." But in his last hours, the miserable sinner cried out to the Lord, and He snapped the chains that bound his soul and set him free. He threw him a passport into heaven. I can imagine, as the soldier drove his spear into our Savior's side, there came flashing into the mind of the thief the words of the prophet Zechariah: *In that time there shall be an open fountain for the house of David and for the inhabitants of Jerusalem against sin and against uncleanness* (Zechariah 13:1).

You can see from the conversion of this thief that salvation is distinct and separate from works. Some people tell us we have to work to be saved. What do those who believe that say about the salvation of this thief? How could he work when he was nailed to the cross? He took the Lord at His word and believed. It is with the heart that people believe – not with their hands or feet. All that is necessary for anyone to be saved is to believe with the heart.

This thief made a good confession. If he had been a Christian for fifty years, he could not have done Christ more service there than he did. He confessed Jesus before the world, and for two thousand years that confession has been told. Luke recorded all of it. He felt it was important that we should know what happened.

See how salvation is separate and distinct from all ordinances. Ordinances are right in their place, but many people think it is impossible for anyone to get into the kingdom of God if he is not baptized into it. I know people who were very disturbed because little children died unbaptized. I have seen them carry the children through the streets because the pastor could not come.

I am not talking against ordinances. Baptism is right in its place, but when you put it in the place of salvation, you put a snare in the way. You cannot baptize people into the kingdom of God. The last conversion before Christ perished on the cross should forever settle that question. If I am told that someone cannot get into heaven without being baptized, I answer, "This thief was not baptized. If he had wanted to be baptized, I don't believe he could have found anyone to baptize him."

I have known people who had sick relatives, but when they could not get a minister to come to their house and administer the sacrament, they became distressed and troubled. I am not speaking against the ordinance by which we commemorate the death of our Lord and remember His return. God forbid! But it is not necessary for salvation. I might die and be lost before I could get to the Lord's Table, but if I get to the Lord, I am saved.

Thank God, salvation is always within my reach, and I don't have to wait for a minister. This poor thief certainly never partook of the Lord's Supper. Was there a man on that hill who would have had faith to believe he was saved? Would any church today have received him into membership? He didn't have to wait for this. The moment he asked for life, our Savior gave it.

Baptism is one thing, the ordinance of the Lord's Supper is another thing, and salvation through Christ is quite another thing. If we have been saved through Christ, let us confess Him by baptism. Let us go to His table and do whatever else He asks; but let us not make stumbling blocks out of these things.

That is what I call sudden conversion – people calling on God for salvation and getting it. You certainly won't get it unless you call for it and unless you take it when He offers it to you. If you want Christ to remember you, to save you – then call upon Him.

Two Sides

The cross of Christ divides all mankind. There are only two sides – those for Christ and those against Him. Think of the two thieves; from the side of Christ, one went down to death cursing God, and the other went to glory.

What a contrast! In the morning the thief was led out as a condemned criminal; in the evening he was saved from his sins. In the morning he was cursing; in the evening he was singing hallelujahs with a choir of angels. In the morning he was condemned by men as not fit to live on earth; in the evening he was considered good enough for heaven. In the morning he was nailed to the cross; in the evening he was in the paradise of God, crowned with a crown he will wear through all the ages. In the morning not an eye pitied him; in the evening the blood of the Lamb washed him and made him clean. In the morning he belonged to the society of thieves and outcasts; in the evening Christ was not ashamed to walk arm-in-arm with him down the golden pavement of the eternal city.

The thief was the first man to enter paradise after the veil of the temple was torn. If we could look up and catch a glimpse of the throne, we would see the Father with Jesus Christ at His right hand, and nearby we would see that thief. He is there today. He has been there for two thousand years, just because he cried in faith: *Lord, remember me when thou comest into thy kingdom.*

Jesus died a little while before the thief. I can imagine that He wanted to hurry home to get a place ready for His new friend, the first soul brought from the world He was dying to redeem. The Lord loved him because he confessed Him in that dark hour. It was a dark hour for many who reviled the Savior. You might have heard of the child who did not want to die and go to heaven because he didn't know anybody there, but the thief would have at least one acquaintance there. I can imagine how his soul leaped within him when he saw the spear thrust into our Savior's side and heard the cry, *It is finished!* (John 19:30).

The thief wanted to follow Christ. When they came to break his legs, he was in a hurry to be gone. I can imagine the Lord calling, "Gabriel, prepare a chariot. Make haste. There is a friend of mine hanging on that cross. They are breaking his legs. He will soon be ready to come. Make haste and bring him to Me." The angel in the chariot swept down from heaven, took the soul of that penitent thief, and hurried back to glory. The gates of the city swung wide open, and the angels shouted to welcome this poor sinner who had been washed spotless in the blood of the Lamb.

That, my friends, is just what Christ wants to do for you. That is the business on which He came down from heaven. That is why He died. If He gave such a swift salvation to this poor thief on the cross, surely He will give you the same if, like the penitent thief, you repent, confess, and trust in the Savior.

Someone might say that this man was saved at the eleventh hour. I don't know about that. It might have been the first hour with him. Perhaps he never knew of Christ until he was led out to die beside Him. This may have been the very first time he had a chance to know the Son of God. How many of you gave your hearts to Christ the very first time He asked you? Are you not further along in the day than even that poor thief?

Some years ago in one of the mining districts of England, a young man attended one of our meetings and refused to leave until he had found peace in the Savior. The next day he went down into the mining pit, and the coal fell in on him. When they brought him out, he was broken and mangled and had only two or three minutes of life left in him. His friends gathered about him and saw his lips moving. Bending down to catch his words, they heard him say, "It was a good thing I settled it last night."

Settle it now, my friends, once for all. Begin now to confess your sins and pray to the Lord to remember you. He will make you an heir of His kingdom if you will accept the gift of salvation. He is the same Savior the thief had. Will you not cry to Him for mercy?

The Dying Thief

A cross, – and one who hangs thereon, in sight
Of heaven and earth.
The cruel nails are fast
In trembling hands and feet, the face is white
And changed with agony, the failing head
Is drooping heavily; but still again,
And yet again, the weary eyes are raised
To seek the face of One who hangeth pale
Upon another cross. He hears no shrill
And taunting voices of the crowd beneath,
He marks no cruel looks of all that gaze
Upon the woeful sight. He sees alone
That face upon the cross. Oh, long, long look,
That searcheth there the deep and awful things
Which are of God!
In his first agony
And horror he had joined with them that spake
Against the Lord, the Lamb, who gave Himself
That day for us. But when he met the look
Of those calm eyes, – he paused that instant; pale
And trembling, stricken to the heart, and faint
At sight of Him.

. . . .

At length
The pale, glad lips have breathed the trembling prayer
"*O Lord, remember me!*" The hosts of God
With wistful angel-faces, bending low
Above their dying King, were surely stirred

To wonder at the cry. Not one of all
The shining host had dared to speak to Him
In that dread hour of woe, when Heaven and Earth
Stood trembling and amazed. Yet, lo! the voice
Of one who speaks to Him, who dares to pray,
"O Lord, remember me!" A sinful man
May make his pitiful appeal to Christ,
The sinner's Friend, when angels dare not speak
And sweetly from the dying lips that day
The answer came.

Oh, strange and solemn joy
Which broke upon the fading face of him
Who there received the promise: *"Thou shalt be
In Paradise this night, this night, with Me."*

. . . .

O Christ, the King!
We also wander on the desert-hills,
Though haunted by Thy call, returning sweet
At morn and eve. We will not come to Thee
Till Thou hast nailed us to some bitter cross.
And *made* us look on Thine, and driven at last
To call on Thee with trembling and with tears, –
Thou lookest down in love, upbraiding not,
And promising the kingdom!

. . . .

A throne, – and one
Who kneels before it, bending low in new
And speechless joy.

It is the night on earth,
The shadows fall like dew upon the hills
Around the Holy City, but above,
Beyond the dark vale of the sky, beyond
The smiling of the stars, they meet once more
In peace and glory. Heaven is comforted, –
For that strange warfare is accomplished now,
Her King returned with joy: and one who watched
The far-off morning in a prison dim,
And hung at noonday on the bitter cross,
Is kneeling at His feet, and tasteth now
The sweet, sweet opening of an endless joy.[6]

6 Barbara Macandrew, excerpts from "The Dying Thief," *Ezekiel and Other Poems* (London: T. Nelson and Sons, Paternoster Row, 1871), 165-176.